CHECK YOUR ENGLISH VOCABULARY FOR

TOEFL®

by

Rawdon Wyatt

BLOOMSBURY

First published in Great Britain 2004 by A & C Black Publishers Ltd

This fourth edition published 2012 by

Bloomsbury Publishing Plc
50 Bedford Square
London
WC1B 3DP
www.bloomsbury.com

A CIP record for this book is available from the British Library.

ISBN: 978-1-4081-5392-5

This book is produced using paper that is made from wood grown in managed, sustainable forests. It is natural, renewable and recyclable. The logging and manufacturing processes conform to the environmental regulations of the country of origin.

Typeset by Saxon Graphics Ltd, Derby
Printed and bound in Great Britain by Martins the Printers

Introduction

Introduction

If you are going to take the TOEFL®, you will find the vocabulary exercises in this workbook very helpful. They will help you to review, practice and acquire a lot of the words and expressions that you might need to use in the Writing and Speaking sections, or that you might come across or be tested on in the Listening and Reading sections. A greater command of vocabulary is one of the key factors that will help you raise your TOEFL® score.

Structure of the workbook

The workbook is divided into two sections. The first section deals with general vocabulary, including synonyms, idioms, and phrasal verbs. The second, smaller section is topic-specific, and focuses on some of the topics that regularly appear in the TOEFL®. Each topic is accompanied by a typical TOEFL® Writing question, which will give you the chance to use the key vocabulary in an essay.
There is a comprehensive answer key at the back of the book.

How to use the book

You should not go through the exercises mechanically. It is better to choose areas that you are unfamiliar with, or areas that you feel are of specific interest or importance to yourself. Remember that you should keep a record of new words and expressions that you learn, and review these from time to time so that they become an active part of your vocabulary. There is a vocabulary record sheet at the back of the book which you can photocopy as many times as you like. Use this to build up your own personal vocabulary bank.
We recommend that you have a good dictionary with you, and refer to it when necessary. However, always try to do the exercises without a dictionary first, and then use the dictionary to check anything that you are not sure of. A particularly useful reference is the *Macmillan English Dictionary for Advanced Learners*. You will find a free on line version of this at www.macmillandictionary.com. When you open the web page, make sure you choose 'American', which you will find by clicking on 'Options' at the top of the page.

Extending your vocabulary

Also remember that there are other methods of acquiring new vocabulary. For example, you should read as much as possible from a different variety of authentic reading materials (books, newspapers, magazines, on line articles, etc.).

Practicing for the TOEFL

There is a lot of TOEFL® material available, but we particularly recommend Barron's *TOEFL® iBT* by Pamela J. Sharpe (ISBN 978-0-7641-9698-0), which provides comprehensive practice for all sections of the exam, as well as offering essential language skills development and useful studying strategies. It also gives lots of vital information on the test itself and how it works. The book has been written for the Internet-based TOEFL®, but is also useful if you are going to take the older, standard computer-based TOEFL®. You might also like to consider

Barron's *Practice Exercises for the TOEFL®* by the same author (ISBN 978-0-7641-4566-7), and *Achieve TOEFL® iBT* by Renald Rilcy and Rawdon Wyatt (ISBN 978-0-462-00447-1).

Information about the TOEFL®

The purpose of the TOEFL® is to evaluate a non-native English speaker's proficiency in the English language. Almost one million students every year from 180 countries register to take the TOEFL®: the majority of universities and colleges in North America as well as in other English-speaking countries require official TOEFL® score reports for admission. The test is also used by institutions in other countries where English is the language of instruction. In addition, government agencies, scholarship programs, and licensing / certification agencies use TOEFL® scores to evaluate English proficiency. An acceptable score depends on the particular institution or agency involved.

About the *Check your English Vocabulary* series

Check your English Vocabulary for TOEFL is one of several books in the *Check your English Vocabulary* series. These books are designed to help students of English (and those who are working or who want to work in an English-speaking environment) to develop and practice the essential vocabulary that they would need to know or use on a day-to-day basis, or in order to get a better grade in an exam.

There are currently 15 books in the series:

Check your English Vocabulary for Academic English
Check your English Vocabulary for TOEFL®
Check your English Vocabulary for TOEIC
Check your English Vocabulary for IELTS
Check your English Vocabulary for FCE+
Check your English Vocabulary for PET
Check your English Vocabulary for Phrasal Verbs and Idioms
Check your English Vocabulary for Business and Administration
Check your English Vocabulary for Law
Check your English Vocabulary for Medicine
Check your English Vocabulary for Computing
Check your English Vocabulary for Leisure, Travel and Tourism
Check your English Vocabulary for Human Resources
Check your English Vocabulary for Banking and Finance
Check your English Vocabulary for Living in the UK

For more information, visit www.acblack.com

Contents

Addition, equation, and conclusion

Put the following words and phrases into their correct place in the table depending on their function. Three of them have been done for you.

along with   also   and   as well as   besides   correspondingly   equally furthermore   in addition   in brief   in conclusion   in the same way likewise   moreover   similarly   therefore   thus   to conclude to summarize   to sum up briefly   too   we can conclude that   what's more

Addition	Equation	Conclusion
and	*equally*	*in conclusion*

Exercise 2

Complete these sentences with one of the words or phrases from above. In most cases, more than one answer is possible.

1. Tourism brings much needed money to developing countries. .... it provides employment for the local population.

2. .... bringing much needed money to developing countries, tourism provides employment for the local population.

3. Tourists should respect the local environment. .... they should respect the local customs.

4. .... industrial waste, pollution from car fumes is poisoning the environment.

5. In order to travel, you need a passport. ...., you might need a visa, immunization jabs, and written permission to visit certain areas.

6. Knives are banned from hand baggage on all flights. .... other sharp objects such as scissors.

7. All power corrupts. ...., absolute power corrupts absolutely.

8. You shouldn't smoke, drink, take drugs, or eat unhealthy food. ...., you should live a more healthy lifestyle.

9. The ozone layer is becoming depleted, the air in the cities is becoming too dirty to breathe and our seas and rivers are no longer safe to swim in. .... pollution is slowly destroying the planet.

10. Your grades have been very poor all year. .... you need to work really hard if you want to pass your exams next month.

This exercise looks at some common 'American' words (words which are used in the United States and Canada). You might find it useful if you have been learning 'British' English (the English which is spoken in the United Kingdom and in other countries around the world). Generally, 'American' words are understood by 'British' English speakers (largely as a result of imported television programs and movies), but many North Americans are unfamiliar with some 'British' English words. As a result, it is important to use the 'American' words rather than the 'British' words in the TOEFL®.

Look at the sentences below, which all contain a 'British' English word in **bold**. Decide what word North Americans would normally use in the same context. In some cases, the word will remain the same, but there will be a difference in spelling. Write your answers in the crossword grid on page 7. To help you, the word that you need has been put at the end of each sentence, with most of the letters removed, but with some of the letters included.

Across (⇨)

2. The play is in two acts, with a short **interval** between the two.   I _ T _ _ M _ _ _ _ _ N

6. If you make a mistake in your calculations, you'll need to do them **again**.   _ V _ _

8. The **post** normally arrives before lunchtime.   _ _ _ L

9. The government refused to **recognise** the new republic.   _ E _ _ _ _ _ _ _

11. The **theatre** received an unexpected grant which helped to prevent it closing down.   _ H _ _ _ _ _

13. The road outside the school is very busy, so students are advised to use the **subway** to cross it.
    _ N _ _ _ P _ _ _

16. The oil crisis resulted in a 28% rise in the cost of **petrol**.   _ _ S

18. Take the **lift** to the top floor.   _ _ _ V _ _ O _

20. **Estate agents** are some of the most unscrupulous people in the country.   R _ _ L _ _ R _

24. The M40 is closed, so you will need to take the A40, which is the **main road** connecting London with Oxford.   H _ _ _ W _ _

26. Their request for a $2 **rise** in the hourly rate was firmly rejected by the management.   _ A _ _ E

27. The workshop will last for six hours, with a **break** for lunch at midday.   _ E _ _ S _

29. (*Informal*) I really like Mr Goldberg. He's a great **bloke**.   _ U _

30. (*At a school, college or university*) A **staff** meeting has been called for two o'clock.   _ _ C _ _ _ Y

32. In my opinion, the best time of the year is **autumn**.   _ _ L _

35. The automobile company's first attempt to design a family **saloon** that ran on diesel was a resounding failure.   _ _ D _ N

36. The campus has a **shop** where students can buy stationery and essential items.   _ _ O _ _

37. Government spending on **defence** was reduced by 23%.   _ _ _ E _ _ _

38. He gave me just enough money to buy a **return** bus ticket to Portland.   R _ _ _ D - _ _ _ P
(two words, which are hyphenated. Do not leave a gap or use a hyphen in the crossword grid)

40. He's a **graduate** of Berkeley College.   (an) _ _ _ M N _ _

41. These days it is not unusual to see children as young as five carrying a **mobile phone** to school.
C _ _ _ _ _ _ N _

Down (⇩)

1. The **postcode** for the company is MA 04532.   _ I _ _ O _ _
(two words: do not leave a gap between the words in the crossword grid)

3. Classes start at nine o'clock every morning Monday **to** Friday.   T _ R _ _ _ _

4. There are several museums and galleries in the city, but most students prefer to spend their evenings
at the **cinema**.   _ _ V _ E _

5. Have you got any change for a $20 **note**?   B _ _ _

7. Strict **labour** laws have had an adverse effect on small businesses.   _ _ B _ _

10. I'm afraid we've **got** slightly behind schedule.   _ _ T T _ _

12. Several **flats** were leased to private agencies, who in turn leased them to small companies.
_ P _ _ T _ _ _ _ _

14. All **travelers** flying to the United States have to undergo strict security checks at the airport.
_ _ A _ _ _ _ _ _

15. The Dean's office is on the **ground** floor.   _ I _ _ _

17. The first thing the council did was dig up the **pavement** outside the front door.   _ _ D _ W _ _ _

19. My favorite **film** of all time has to be the classic 1959 comedy *Some Like It Hot*.   _ _ V _ _

21. The best way to get from one part of the city to another is to use the **dual carriageway**.
_ _ E _ W _ _

22. (*On the telephone, when you are calling someone*) Hello, is **that** Harrison Keane?   _ _ _ S

23. In the event of a marital divorce or separation, there is a clear need for **dialogue** between the
parents and their children.   _ _ A _ _ _

25. If you want to stop smoking, the best place to start is by going to your local **chemist**.
D _ _ G _ _ _ _ _

28. Services on the **underground** start at five in the morning and finish at half past midnight.
_ _ B _ _ Y

31. Before buying a house, it is essential to employ the services of a good **solicitor**.   _ T T _ _ _ _ _

33. You should use a pencil to do the test, and use a **rubber** to remove any mistakes.   _ _ A _ _ _

34. Most Americans tend to stay in the country for their **holiday**.   V _ _ _ T _ _ _

39. You don't need to ask me for permission to use the **toilet**!   B _ _ _ R _ _ _

Changes

Exercise 1

Look at these sentences and decide if the statement which follows each one is <u>true</u> (**T**) or <u>false</u> (**F**). Use the words and phrases in **bold** to help you decide.

1.   The population of the country has trebled in the last 25 years.
        *There has been a **dramatic increase** in the number of people living in the country.* **T / F**

2.   Unemployment has dropped by about 2% every year for the last six years.
        *There has been a **steady decrease** in the number of people out of work.* **T / F**

3.   In the last six months, the government has improved the national road system.
        *There has been a **deterioration** in the national road system.* **T / F**

4.   The number of exam passes achieved by the school's pupils has risen by almost 50%.
        *There has been a **decline** in the number of exam passes.* **T / F**

5.   American travelers abroad have discovered that they can buy more foreign currency with their dollar.
        *There has been a **weakening** of the dollar.* **T / F**

6.   It is now much easier to visit the country than it was a few years ago.
        *There has been a **tightening up** of border controls.* **T / F**

7.   We're increasing our stocks of coal before the winter begins.
        *We're **running down** our stocks of coal.* **T / F**

8.   Food prices have gone up by about 4% every year since 2004.
        *There has been a **constant rise** in the price of food since 2004.* **T / F**

9.   The pass rate for the exam was 3% lower this year than it was last year.
        *There has been a **sharp fall** in the pass rate.* **T / F**

10.   The Southern Alliance is going to reduce the number of conventional weapons in their armed forces.
        *The Southern Alliance is going to **build up** the number of conventional weapons in their armed forces.* **T / F**

11.   Deflation has adversely affected industries around the country.
        *There has been a **growth** in industrial activity.* **T / F**

12.   The rules regarding smoking in public places are much stricter now than they were before.
        *There has been a **relaxation** of the rules regarding smoking in public places.* **T / F**

13.   Last year, 12% of the population worked in industry and 10% worked in agriculture. This year, 14% of the population work in industry and 8% work in agriculture.
        *There has been a **narrowing of the gap** between those working in different sectors of the economy.* **T / F**

14.   Some management roles in the company will not exist this time next year.
        *Some management roles are going to be **phased out**.* **T / F**

15.   These days, more people shop at large supermarkets than in small local stores.
        *There has been an **upward trend** in the number of people shopping in small local stores.* **T / F**

16.   Her English is clearly better now than it was when she first arrived.
        *There has been **marked progress** in her English.* **T / F**

17.   People live in better houses, drive nicer cars, and eat better-quality food than they did 20 years ago.
        *There has been a **general improvement** in the standard of living in the last 20 years.* **T / F**

18.   Our company has opened several new offices in the last five years.
        *Our company has witnessed **considerable expansion** in the last five years.* **T / F**

19.   The government will spend less on the healthcare services next year.
        *There are going to be **cuts** in healthcare spending next year.* **T / F**

20.   Americans nowadays want to see more of the world.
        *Americans nowadays want to **narrow** their horizons.* **T / F**

Exercise 2

The box below contains 31 more words used to describe change in different situations. These are all verbs, and they can be found by reading from left to right and from right to left, starting in the top-left corner and following the direction of the arrows. Separate these words, then use some of them to complete sentences 1 – 10 below. In some cases you will need to change the form of the verb (for example, by putting it into its past simple or past participle form).

⇨	a	d	a	p	t	r	e	p	l	a	c	e	e	x	p	a	n	d	p	r	⇗
⇖	m	r	o	f	s	n	a	r	t	e	c	u	d	e	r	e	t	o	m	o	⇙
⇘	s	w	i	t	c	h	r	e	n	o	v	a	t	e	e	x	c	h	a	n	⇗
⇖	e	p	p	a	s	i	d	r	e	t	l	a	e	t	o	m	e	d	e	g	⇙
⇘	a	r	v	a	r	y	r	a	i	s	e	l	o	w	e	r	e	x	t	e	⇗
⇖	n	e	l	n	e	t	h	g	i	e	h	e	g	r	a	l	n	e	d	n	⇙
⇘	g	t	h	e	n	d	e	e	p	e	n	s	h	o	r	t	e	n	s	t	⇗
⇖	o	t	u	c	d	n	e	m	a	e	s	i	v	e	r	h	c	t	e	r	⇙
⇘	u	t	s	o	u	r	c	e	d	e	t	e	r	i	o	r	a	t	e	s	⇗
⇖	t	s	e	r	e	d	a	r	g	p	u	e	n	i	l	m	a	e	r	t	⇙
⇘	r	u	c	t	u	r	e	d	o	w	n	s	i	z	e			**END**			

1. The company cannot refund customers' money, and goods can only be .... on production of a receipt or other proof of purchase.

2. We have made radical changes to college regulations, and students are expected to .... to these over the next few weeks.

3. The discovery of oil .... the country from a small emirate to a major economic power.

4. The Science block is currently being ...., but will remain open while building work is carried out.

5. After only three weeks on the History course, she decided to .... to something more practical.

6. Fees .... according to the length of the course: the longer the course, the more you pay.

7. As water freezes, it ....

8. The economic situation is .... rapidly, and the entire economy is in danger of collapse.

9. Course fees will be .... on January 14: some will come down, but most of them will go up.

10. Elastic becomes weaker the more it is ....

Comparing and Contrasting

Choose the most appropriate word or phrase in **bold** in these sentences. In one case, all three options are possible.

1. The **contrast / compare / comparison** in working conditions between our Denver department and our department in Chicago is very noticeable, and employees are now demanding equality in this area.

2. The two engines **differentiate / differ / different** considerably from each other: one runs on gasoline, and the other is a gasoline-electric hybrid.

3. It is often difficult to **differentiate / differ / contrast** between students who are absent because they are genuinely sick, and those who are just enjoying a day in bed.

4. The new software program shared some common **characters / characterises / characteristics** with those that were already on the market.

5. There's a clear **distinguish / distinctive / distinction** between studying at a college and working from home on a distance-learning course.

6. **Compared / Compare / Comparing** with just 10 years ago, home PCs are cheaper, faster and have a much bigger memory.

7. The two courses are different in every way: there's absolutely no **compare / comparison / contrast** between them.

8. Our digital photography course is **similar to / alike / resemble** our traditional photography course, except that it is obviously more computer-oriented.

9. There were several **similarities / similarly / similar to** between the two novels, except one was aimed at a younger market while the other targeted adults.

10. Experienced computer hackers can access your personal files and destroy or alter them. **Exactly / In the same way / Just as**, they can gain access to your Internet banking facility and steal your money.

11. The quality of his work is excellent. **Likewise / Alike / Likeness**, his attitude and commitment.

12. The TOEFL® has a variety of academic and general English tasks. **In contrast to / Although / By way of contrast**, the TOEIC focuses more on business and professional issues.

13. Grades have not been good over the last semester. **Nevertheless / Even so / However**, the college still has one of the best academic records in the state.

14. There currently seems to be a large **discrepancy / discrimination / differential** between the number of people employed in service industries, and those employed in the primary sector.

15. The Impressionists used light and color to give the general feeling of a scene, **unlike / whereas / whereby** the pre-Raphaelites used a lot of detail and bright colors, and depicted a romanticized view of life.

Condition and requirement

Rearrange the letters in **bold** to make words and phrases related to condition and requirement. The first one has been done as an example.

1. **sa nlgo sa** there is sufficient demand for healthy food such as salads and soups in the school cafeteria, we will continue to provide it.
    (**Answer = *As long as***)

2. **seusln** I receive your assignment within the next couple of days, I will have to give you a lower grade for the course.   ....

3. Students may use the college computers for personal emails **no incotnido atth** they agree to give up their computer if someone needs it for coursework.   ....

4. Everyone should get a good mid-term grade **vogrnipid ttha** they hand in all their work on time.   ....

5. The main **retncopiinsod** for a healthy economy are controlled consumer spending and low unemployment.   ....

6. (Notice on a fire alarm): **ni eacs fo** fire, break glass.   ....

7. **ni het nvete fo** a draw between the two teams in tonight's game, there will be a replay on Saturday afternoon.   ....

8. We agreed to sign the contract, the only **aputonstili** being that it would run for at least five years.   ....

9. The teachers have **nidncoalitoun** trust in their students: they know they will do their best at all times, even if things get difficult.   ....

10. **sumsagin hatt** the flight is on time, we will meet you at LaGuardia airport at ten o'clock.
    ....

11. His argument was based **no teh autonmsspi hatt** people are basically decent and honest.
    ....

12. Good language skills are one of the **quereesisitpr** for a job in an international organization.
    ....

13. Before you accept a job, it is important that you agree with the **remst** and **ioctnsodin** set out in the contract.   ....

14. It is a **nmreiretque** of the college that students attend at least 90% of their course and complete all their assignments on time.   ....

15. If you have a query, please telephone us at the number above. **niifagl ttha**, send us an email.
    ....

16. We need to involve at least 20 people on this project, **ehewotris** it can't go ahead.
    ....

Confusing words

<u>Confusing words</u> are two or more words which have a similar meaning to each other but are used in a different way.
or
are related to the same topic, but have a different meaning
or
look similar, but have a different meaning

Complete the following sentences with the appropriate word in **bold**.

1.   **action / activity**
     We decided to take immediate .... when we realized there was a problem.
     The environmental changes in the area are the result of human ....

2.   **advice / advise**
     Can you .... me on the best course of action to take?
     He offered me some excellent ....

3.   **affect / effect**
     Diverting the course of the river will have a major .... on the local ecosystem.
     Frequent traffic jams in the suburbs seriously .... journey times into the city.

4.   **alternative / alternate**
     If our teachers are ill and have to take a day off work, the college usually does its best to make .... arrangements.
     During the vacation, the college doctor is only on site on .... days (Monday, Wednesday, and Friday).

5.   **appreciable / appreciative**
     Widening the road made an .... difference to the flow of traffic.
     The applause at the end of the concert was warm and ....

6.   **assumption / presumption**
     They raised taxes on the .... that it would help control spending.
     It's sheer .... for the government to suggest things have improved since they came to power.

7.   **avoid / prevent**
     Rapid international action managed to .... an environmental disaster from taking place.
     There are areas in the city that are wise to .... visiting after dark.

8.   **beside / besides**
     The office is just .... the bus station.
     .... their regular daytime job, many people do extra work in the evening.

9.   **briefly / shortly**
     .... before the earthquake began, many animals were seen to be behaving in an unusual manner.
     She spoke .... but passionately about the need to help those in developing countries.

10. **canal / channel**
     A .... system joined the two main rivers, which made transporting goods much quicker.
     When television first became popular in the early 1950s, most viewers only had access to one ....

11. **complimentary / complementary**
In western societies, acupuncture and hypnosis are seen as .... medicines.
All new students will receive a .... study pack and dictionary.

12. **conscientious / conscious**
Most people are .... of the need to protect the environment.
.... workers should be rewarded for their hard work.

13. **continual / continuous**
The computer system has given us .... problems ever since we installed it. Some days it works, other days it doesn't.
The .... noise from the new freeway has forced many people to move.

14. **control / inspect**
New teachers often find it difficult to .... their classes.
Environmental health inspectors regularly .... commercial kitchens for cleanliness, especially those in restaurants.

15. **criticism / objection**
I have no .... to people using their cellphones on buses or trains.
Plans for the new stadium have attracted fierce .... from local people.

16. **damage / harm / injury**
He suffered a serious .... which needed immediate hospital treatment.
The low levels of dangerous chemicals in the river were enough to .... aquatic life.
A lot of .... was caused to buildings along the coast during the storm.

17. **disinterested / uninterested**
In order to end the dispute, we need some impartial advice from a / an .... third party.
I thought they would enjoy my talk, but they were completely ....

18. **during / for / while**
The college closes .... two weeks at the end of December.
He died .... trying to cross the desert alone.
Many creatures stay underground .... daylight hours.

19. **however / moreover**
The plan was good in theory. ...., in practice it was extremely difficult to implement.
The plan was excellent. ...., it was clear from the beginning that it was going to be a success.

20. **imply / infer**
From what you just said, can I .... that you think I'm interfering?
I didn't mean to .... that you were interfering. I merely said that I needed a bit of time to myself.

21. **injured / wounded**
I believe that we should do more to help and support soldiers who have been .... in combat.
Several workers were .... when the drilling platform collapsed.

22. **job / work**
Everybody has the right to a decent .... with good pay.
During the economic recession, a lot of people found themselves out of ....

23. **lay / lie**

If you're suffering from dehydration, you should drink plenty of water and sit or .... down for a while.

Before you begin the experiment, you should .... a large plastic sheet on the ground.

24. **look at / watch**

We need to .... the situation carefully over the next few weeks and see how things develop.

We need to .... the problem carefully and decide if there is anything we can do about it.

25. **percent / percentage**

It is a myth that only 10 .... of Americans hold a passport.

Only a small .... of land is privately owned.

26. **permission / permit**

I'm afraid we can't .... photography in here.

We received .... to attend the meeting as long as we didn't interrupt.

27. **possibility / chance**

We might go to Niagara Falls for our field trip. Another .... is that we'll go to Yellowstone instead.

If we act now, we have a good .... of finding a cure for the disease.

28. **priceless / worthless**

.... paintings by artists like Van Gogh and Rembrandt should not be in the hands of private collectors.

As inflation spiraled out of control, paper money suddenly became ....

29. **principal / principle**

Many people refuse to eat meat on ....

She was appointed University .... in 2009.

The country's .... food products are coffee and sugar.

I believe in the .... that healthcare should be free for everyone.

30. **problem / trouble**

At night, the streets are full of people fighting and generally causing ....

I was wondering if you could help me with a little .... I'm having.

31. **raise / rise**

As prices ...., demand usually drops.

In response to the current oil shortage, most airlines had to .... their fares.

32. **remember / remind**

I can .... my first day at school really well.

Language teachers often .... their students that the best way to remember new words is to use them as much as possible.

33. **subjective / objective**

Your report should be as .... as possible: just present the facts and try to avoid saying what you think about them.

The newspaper article was extremely ....: the journalist more or less forced his own views and ideas on his readership.

34. **tolerable / tolerant**

People need to be more .... of their neighbors, and not complain every time they make too much noise.

The local authorities say that the noise from passing trains is ...., but many living near the railroad lines disagree.

35. **treat / cure**

Hospitals are so understaffed that they find it almost impossible to .... patients with minor injuries.

They were unable to .... the disease, and hundreds died as a result.

Idioms and colloquialisms 1

Idioms and colloquialisms (spoken expressions) are a common feature of the TOEFL® Listening Comprehension. There are a lot of them, and each one has to be learnt individually. Often, but not always, it is possible to identify the meaning of an idiom or a colloquialism from the context in which it is being used.

The idioms and colloquialisms exercises in this book focus on some of the most commonly used expressions.

Exercise 1
Complete each dialog with an appropriate expression from the box.

Can I take a rain check on that?   I couldn't agree more.   I couldn't care less.
I really don't mind. It's up to you.   It does nothing for me.   Let me sleep on it.
Never mind. It can't be helped.   Why not? Go for it!   Wow! Way to go!
You should really get a life.   You're welcome, but it was nothing really.
You've got to be kidding!

1.   A. Shall we eat out or do you want me to cook something?
      B. ....
      A. OK. In that case, let's eat out.

2.   A. The economics seminar has been canceled yet again.
      B. ....
      A. I'm afraid not. Professor Parkhill sure seems to be absent a lot these days.

3.   A. Our history lessons are really boring, aren't they.
      B. ....
      A. Right. Perhaps we shouldn't have chosen it as an option.

4.   A. We're going to Sam's bar tonight. Want to come?
      B. ....
      A. Sure. Perhaps at the weekend?

5.   A. I need a decision as soon as possible.
      B. ....
      A. Well, to be honest, I'd rather you told me now.

6.   A. Are you interested in science?
      B. ....
      A. Me neither. I find it really boring.

7.   A. I spent most of the weekend lying in bed and watching TV.
      B. ....
      A. I know! You're not the first person to say that.

8.   A. If you don't work harder, you'll fail your exams.
      B. ....
      A. Well, you should. Your whole future might depend on them.

9.   A. I've passed all my exams – grade A's all round!
      B. ....
      A. Thanks. I never thought I'd be able to do it.

10.   A. Do you think I should apply to the University of West Virginia?
      B. ....
      A. All right, I will. Thanks.

11.   A. Thank you so much for all your help. I couldn't have done it without you.
      B. ....
      A. No, really, I really appreciate it.

12.   A. I'm really sorry that I lost your dictionary.
      B. ....
      A. Nevertheless, I promise to replace it.

Now do the same with these:

Let me lend a hand.　　How's it going?　　How should I know? Sorry, I'm a bit tied up right now.　　I'm afraid you're out of luck. I'm going to give it all I've got.　　Is it any wonder?　　Oh, I'm used to it. Sure. Why not?　　What a drag!　　What do you have in mind?　　You bet!

1.　　A. Can I have a look at your essay to get a few ideas?
　　　　B. ....
　　　　A. Thanks. I'll do the same for you next time.

2.　　A. I'm working really hard for my exam at the moment.
　　　　B. ....
　　　　A. Oh, not bad. I'm fairly confident of passing.

3.　　A. Where's Murai today?
　　　　B. ....
　　　　A. Don't be like that. I was only asking.

4.　　A. We need to finish this assignment by Monday. There goes our weekend.
　　　　B. ....
　　　　A. I know, but we'll make up for it next weekend.

5.　　A. Want to come to the concert tonight?
　　　　B . ...
　　　　A. That's great. I'll go and get us some tickets.

6.　　A. Do you think you'll pass your exams?
　　　　B. ....
　　　　A. That's the spirit! Well, good luck.

7.　　A. Do you find it difficult getting up at six o'clock every morning?
　　　　B. ....
　　　　A. I suppose you must be. You've been doing it for so long.

8.　　A. We're thinking of doing something to celebrate the end of the semester.
　　　　B. ....
　　　　A. I'm not sure, really. Perhaps a barbecue, or something like that.

9.　　A. Are there any tickets left for tonight's show?
　　　　B. ....
　　　　A. I thought so. Oh well, never mind.

10.　　A. I have to get the hall ready for tonight's lecture.
　　　　B. ....
　　　　A. That's really kind of you.

11.　　A. I was wondering if you could help me with my assignment.
　　　　B. ....
　　　　A. Yes, I thought you might be a bit busy right now.

12.　　A. Poor Sarah failed to get a good grade in her TOEFL® once again.
　　　　B. ....
　　　　A. Right. She never seems to do any preparation for it.

Idioms and colloquialisms 2

Exercise 1
Complete these dialogs with an appropriate expression from the box.

A little bird told me.   Be my guest.   Fire away, I'm all ears.   I'd be glad to. I'm having second thoughts.   I'm keeping my fingers crossed. My lips are sealed.   Now you're talking!   Rather you than me. That'll be the day!   That'll teach you!   Who let the cat out of the bag?

1.　A. Would you look after my bag while I go to the rest room?
　　B. Sure. ....

2.　A. Do you mind if I sit here?
　　B. Not at all. ....

3.　A. How did you know it was my birthday today?
　　B. Aha!...

4.　A. I'd be really grateful if you didn't tell anyone about my little secret.
　　B. .... I won't breathe a word.

5.　A. Do you think you'll pass the exam?
　　B. I don't know. ....

6.　A. I've signed up for extra Sociology classes with Professor Dullman.
　　B. .... He's so boring!

7.　A. I've got some really interesting news. Do you want to hear it?
　　B. Yes. ....

8.　A. You don't want to work tonight? OK, let's go to the theater instead.
　　B. Great! ....

9.　A. I thought you were going to apply for a place on the Theory of Knowledge course.
　　B. Well, I was. ....

10.　A. I promise to work harder from now on.
　　B. Yeah, right! ....

11.　A. I hear that you're going to throw a surprise party for my birthday.
　　B. .... It's supposed to be a secret.

12.　A. I've just eaten six hot dogs, and now I've got a terrible stomach ache.
　　B. .... You won't do that again in a hurry.

Exercise 2
Instructions as above.

Congratulations.   Couldn't be better.   Hold on.   I'd love to. I'd rather you didn't.   It doesn't ring any bells.   Make yourself at home. Take care and keep in touch.   That's too bad.   This is on me. Yes, knock on wood.   You're welcome.

1.　A. I can't afford to go to the concert tonight.
　　B. I wasn't expecting you to pay. ....

2.　A. I've managed to get a place on the Advanced Studies program.
　　B. .... That's quite an achievement.

3.　A. Would you like to come to Gino's tonight for dinner?
　　B. .... What time?

4.　A. Thank you very much for all your help.
　　B. Not at all. ....

5.　A. Oh wow! What a great room. It's wonderful.
　　B. Thanks. ....

6. A. Hurry up, or we'll miss the start of the movie.
    B. .... I'm not ready yet.

7. A. It's been nice seeing you again. Let's get together again soon.
    B. Yes, definitely. ....

8. A. Hi, Tom. How are you?
    B. Oh, great. ....

9. A. Do you mind if I smoke in here?
    B. .... Anyway, smoking's banned on campus.

10. A. I didn't do too well in the end of semester exams.
    B. Oh, bad luck. ....

11. A. Have you ever heard of the Darwin Awards?
    B. I don't think so. ....

12. A. Do you think you'll do well in tomorrow's test?
    B. .... I've done plenty of revision.

Exercise 3
Instructions as above.

Don't kill yourself.   Gesundheit!   Have a good time.   How's it going?   I'll say.   Not on your life!   It's not the end of the world.   So I guess you're in the doghouse again.   Sure thing.   Take a seat.   That's a load off my mind.   Well, keep it to yourself.

1. A. I'm about halfway through my essay.
    B. Oh good. ....

2. A. I thought the lecture on the Declaration of Independence was great. Did you enjoy it?
    B. .... It was fascinating.

3. A. Snake is considered a delicacy in some countries. Would you ever consider eating it?
    B. Oh yuck! ....

4. A. Professor de Gruchy has extended the deadline for our essays to Thursday.
    B. .... I have so much to do.

5. A. Look, I just found the question paper for tomorrow's test lying on the floor!
    B. .... It can be our secret.

6. A. Could you give me a bit of help with this assignment?
    B. .... What's the problem?

7. A. Can I come in?
    B. Of course. ....

8. A. I've got so much to do by Monday; two essays to write, a presentation to prepare, and I have to do some research on the history of the UN.
    B. That's a lot of work. ....

9. A. I'm so depressed. That's the third time I've failed my driving test.
    B. Never mind. .... Better luck next time.

10. A. I'm off to Niagara Falls for the weekend. See you Monday.
    B. Sure. ....

11. A. I forgot my boyfriend's birthday last week.
    B. Oh dear. ....

12. A. Aaachoooooooo!
    B. .... Have you got a cold?

Idioms and colloquialisms 3

Exercise 1
Connect the first part of each sentence in the first box with the second half in the second box. Use the phrases in **bold** to help you make the connection.

1.	The project was **more or**…
2.	I just need to complete this essay, and then my coursework will be over **once and**…
3.	His lectures are generally really dull, but **once in**…
4.	I've never been **too**…
5.	There are parts of the course which are a bit boring, but **on the**…
6.	Don't try to do everything at once. Try to do things **step by**…
7.	There's a chance that **sooner or**…
8.	When you first start a new job, it can take a while to **learn the**…
9.	I know you have a lot of work, but **look on the bright** …
10.	The President can't be **in his right**…
11.	You shouldn't **go over his**…
12.	You're kidding. You're **pulling my**…

A.	…**big** on science; I've always preferred the arts.
B.	…**side**; at least you won't get bored this weekend!
C.	…**step** until you've finished.
D.	…**a while** there's something of interest.
E.	…**less** complete when someone pointed out they had missed some details.
F.	…**head** and make your own decisions.
G.	…**ropes** and become familiar with the way things work.
H.	…**leg**. Right?
I.	…**later** people will demand some real changes.
J.	…**for all**. It'll be a real relief.
K.	…**mind**, making a stupid decision like that.
L.	…**whole** it's really good.

Exercise 2

Now do the same with these.

1. It can be difficult to **make ends**…

2. Try to **make the most of your**…

3. I asked Ron to get the computer fixed, and he promised to **take**…

4. I understand the theory, but I **get mixed**…

5. Don't worry about the exam. Just **give it**…

6. I'm not sure whether to take a vacation this summer. I'll decide **one way or**…

7. I wasn't sure whether to apply for a PhD course, but in the end I decided to **go**…

8. I got a distinction for my first assignment of the year. That's **a good**…

9. For years he was ignored, then **all at**…

10. Many people believe that it's **about**…

11. I've **changed**…

12. He had some excellent plans, but they never really **got off**…

A. …**for it** and see what happens.

B. …**the ground**.

C. …**time** when you're in New York.

D. …**start**, isn't it?

E. …**all you've got** and hope for the best.

F. …**once**, people began paying attention to what he had to say.

G. …**time** more money was invested in education.

H. …**my mind** about attending Professor Clayton's course.

I. …**up** when I try to describe it on paper.

J. …**the other** when I see my exam results.

K. …**care of** it at the earliest opportunity.

L. …**meet** when you're a student on a limited budget.

Idioms and colloquialisms 4

Exercise 1

Choose the correct <u>underlined</u> word to complete each of the idioms in **bold**. The meaning of each idiom is in *italics* after the sentence.

1. You shouldn't try to **burn the <u>match / lighter / candle</u> at both ends**; you'll exhaust yourself. (*to get up early in the morning and go to bed late at night on a regular basis*)

2. Once he started looking into the details, he realized what **a can of <u>worms / beans / beer</u>** they were opening. (*a difficult and complicated situation*)

3. It was a difficult decision, but he decided to take the **<u>goat / cow / bull</u> by the horns** and tell his boss that he wanted to leave the company. (*to deal bravely or confidently with a difficult situation*)

4. Some insurance companies make their customers **pay through the <u>ears / nose / mouth</u>** for their services. (*pay a lot of money*)

5. He knew that what they were doing was wrong, but **turned a <u>blind / closed / cold</u> eye** to it. (*to pretend not to notice, to ignore*)

6. Many people like to get **off the beaten <u>road / path / track</u>** when they take a vacation. (*somewhere quiet, where not a lot of people go*)

7. If you're **<u>pressed / crushed / squeezed</u> for time**, we can talk later. (*busy, in a hurry*)

8. I've been feeling a bit **under the <u>thumb / weather / table</u>** recently, but I'm feeling better now. (*slightly ill*)

9. He's a rather boring person, but **once in a <u>blue / red / green</u> moon**, he'll come out with something really amazing. (*very rarely*)

10. I'm afraid your request is **out of the <u>answer / statement / question</u>**. (*not possible, unacceptable*)

11. He gave us some information that was strictly **off the <u>books / record / list</u>**. (*unofficial, to be kept secret*)

12. We don't want to **lose <u>land / ground / place</u>** in the baseball competition. (*becomes less successful than the others*)

13. Let's have a party at the beginning of the year. It will help to **break the <u>ice / mold / air</u>**. (*to make people feel more friendly and willing to talk to each other*)

14. Everybody should say exactly how they feel. That should **clear the <u>room / air / feelings</u>**. (*to help end an argument or disagreement*)

15. It's very rude to **talk <u>shop / work / jobs</u>** when you're out with other people. (*to discuss your job with a colleague, usually in a social situation where there are others present*)

16. Don't let him stop you; **stand your <u>land / place / ground</u>** and tell him you won't change your mind. (*refuse to change your mind about something, even when people oppose you*)

17. I only just passed my exam. It was a very **<u>far / close / exact</u> thing**. (*something almost did or didn't happen*)

18. What's happened? **Put me in the <u>picture / story / scene</u>**. (*to let somebody know what has happened, usually when other people already know*)

Exercise 2

Now do the same with these:

1. You've really **made a <u>name / title / place</u> for yourself**, haven't you? (*to become well known, famous and / or respected*)

2. Have you seen his house? It's **out of this <u>planet / earth / world</u>**. (*extremely good, wonderful, etc.*)

3. He knew I was friendly with his boss, and asked me to **pull a few <u>legs / strings / ropes</u>** for him. (*to use your influence with somebody in order to get something*)

4. Donna **<u>played / did / went</u> hooky** again today; that's the third lecture she's missed this week. (*to miss a lesson, class, etc., for no good reason*)

5. My bank account's **in the <u>black / red / pink</u>** again. (*to owe money to the bank because you've spent too much*)

6. I've completed three out of my five assignments already. **So far, so <u>good / fine / acceptable</u>**. (*until now, everything is going well*)

7. I'm really angry with Jerry. It's time I **had it <u>in / out / over</u>** with him. (*to tell somebody you are angry with them, and explain why*)

8. His theories **broke fresh <u>earth / ground / land</u>** and changed the way people thought about science. (*to do something original or innovative*)

9. He said that he had missed his lecture because he had to visit a sick relative, but I don't really think he was **on the <u>air/ ground / level</u>**. (*being honest and telling the truth*)

10. It wasn't my fault! Why am I always the one to **carry the <u>can / tin / box</u>**? (*being the person who is considered responsible for something that has gone wrong*)

11. University life can seem strange at first, but my advice is to **go with the <u>snow / flow / glow</u>** and see what happens. (*to do what seems the easiest thing in a particular situation*)

12. I thought my last essay was really good, so old Professor Clack really **rained on my <u>show / carnival / parade</u>** when he told me he thought it was terrible. (*to spoil something or make it much less enjoyable*)

13. The Dean has told me that unless I **turn over a new <u>leaf / book / paper</u>**, I might be asked to leave the course. (*to change your life by starting to be a better person or stopping a bad habit*)

14. There are some good restaurants nearby that **won't <u>bankrupt / break / rob</u> the bank**. (*not expensive*)

15. I can't talk to you now, I'm afraid. I'm **<u>running / walking / jumping</u> a bit late**. (*to be slightly later than normal*)

16. He can be a bit unfriendly, but **by and <u>big / large / huge</u>** he's OK. (*generally*)

17. All right, everyone. We've achieved a lot in the last hour or so. Let's **take <u>three / four / five</u>**. (*to have a short break*)

18. I don't know exactly what he's up to, but my **<u>fifth / sixth / seventh</u> sense** tells me he trying to get out of doing his assignment. (*a special ability to feel things that you cannot see, hear, touch, smell, or taste*)

Metaphors

A metaphor is a word or phrase that means one thing and is used to refer to another thing in order to emphasize their similar qualities. For example, in the sentence '*Picasso was the father of the Cubist movement*', the word *father* is not used in its usual sense to mean someone's male parent. It means that Picasso was the person who started the Cubist movement, or that he was the first one to do it successfully. *Father* is being used in a *metaphorical* way.

Exercise 1: achievements, ideas, and theories
Metaphorically, *achievements*, *ideas*, and *theories* are often seen as *buildings*, with an idea or the process of achieving something being similar to the process of building, and the failure of something being similar to the destruction of a building. Metaphorically, ideas are also like *plants*, and developing an idea is like getting plants to grow.

Complete sentences 1 – 20 with a word or phrase from the box. In several cases you will need to change the form of the words. The first one has been done for you.

architect	blueprint	build on	build up	buttress	collapse	construct
deep-rooted	demolish	~~edifice~~	fertile	fruitful	ground-breaking	
lay the foundations	ruins	sow the seeds	stem from	take root		
towering	under construction					

1. The newspaper article threatened the whole ....*edifice*........ of government, from the President all the way down to grass-roots politicians.

2. The company Directors were convinced people would want their new product, but then early research and negative feedback began to .... of doubt in their minds.

3. His argument was carefully .... and was extremely difficult to dispute.

4. Her ideas were carefully .... by a series of results showing that they had been put into practice and actually worked.

5. Superstitious beliefs are .... in many cultures, and nothing can change these beliefs.

6. He was the chief .... of the country's new economic policies.

7. The new government .... for radical changes to the health service, all of which would be implemented over the next five years.

8. The invention of the microchip was a .... achievement.

9. The contract acted as a .... for future cooperation between the two organizations.

10. The business was started in 1986, and over the next 20 years was .... into one of the most powerful companies in the country.

11. The new constitution was .... traditional values and a desire for progress.

12. The Web site is ...., but we hope to have it up and running by the end of the month.

13. The idea seemed good in theory, but .... when practical tests were first carried out.

14. The new technology was revolutionary and ...., but was initially seen as a simple novelty.

15. His life's work was in ...., but it did not deter him from starting again.

16. I put forward several ideas, but to my anger and disappointment each one was comprehensively .... by the board.

17. His books were very popular because he had a .... imagination and a talent for telling a good story.

18. Nobody believed him at first, but a series of unexplained events meant that his ideas quickly .... and people were more prepared to listen to him.

19. Her ideas .... her belief in the existence of life on other planets.

20. The discussion was very ...., and we all came away from it believing that at last we were going to achieve something worthwhile.

Exercise 2: Other metaphors.

Look at sentences A, B, and C in the following groups, and look especially at the words and phrases in **bold**. Then complete the final sentence so that it explains what the metaphors in the three sentences are describing. Use the words in the box.

---

argument   discussion   discover   effort   enthusiasm   excitement   failure
force   help   important   intelligence   knowledge   life   opportunity
problem   successful   unimportant

---

1. (A) Your point of view is **indefensible**.
    (B) There was a lot of **conflict** over what to do next.
    (C) The team **clashed** over what steps to take next.

    Metaphorically, an ....*argument*.......... is like a fight or a war, with people 'attacking' and 'defending'.

2. (A) She was one of the **brightest** students in the class.
    (B) As a child, Einstein was believed to have a rather **dull** mind.
    (C) She had a sudden **flash** of inspiration and began writing down her thoughts.

    Metaphorically, ... is like a light. The more you have, the brighter the light is.

3. (A) I was wondering if I could rely on your **support**.
    (B) Would you mind **lending** me a **hand** with my assignment?
    (C) The government helped to **prop up** the college by offering it a financial grant.

    Metaphorically, when you .... someone, it is like supporting them physically (for example, with your body).

4. (A) He is often regarded as the **greatest** writer of the twentieth century.
    (B) Everyone agreed that there were some **weighty** issues to be discussed at the meeting.
    (C) The novel received some good reviews, but many people thought it was rather **lightweight**.

    Metaphorically, something that is .... is like something that is big or heavy, and something that is .... is small or light.

5. (A) They only succeeded by using their political **muscle**.
    (B) She didn't have the **backbone** to accept his challenge.
    (C) I know it's difficult, but you have to **put your back into** it if you want to succeed.

    Metaphorically, making a / an .... is like using a part of your body.

6. (A) You look confused: let me **throw some light on** the matter.
    (B) Her work greatly **illuminated** this aspect of the subject.
    (C) I don't want to be **kept in the dark**, so please let me know what is happening.

    Metaphorically, when you have .... about something, it is like shining a light on it (and when you lack this, it is like being in darkness).

7. (A) His new career **opened the door** to a whole new way of life.
    (B) Having a university degree is arguably the **key** to success in life.
    (C) Age should be **no barrier** to success.

    Metaphorically, having the .... to do something is like having a door or other entrance opened for you.

8. (A) We **unearthed** some useful facts and figures.
    (B) Her latest book is a **goldmine** of useful information.
    (C) We **left no stone unturned** in our search for the truth.

    Metaphorically, when you .... things such as facts and information, it is similar to finding them by digging or searching in the ground.

9. (A) He originally **set out** to become a priest, but became involved in politics instead.
    (B) At the age of 24, things **took an unexpected turn** for him.
    (C) After six years in the same job, I decided to **move on**.

    Metaphorically, ... is like a journey.

10. (A) They put a lot of **pressure** on him to make change his mind.
    (B) The country was **dragged** reluctantly into war.
    (C) I'm sorry to **press** you for an answer, but we need to know your plans.

    Metaphorically, when you .... someone to do something, it is like putting physical pressure on them (for example, by pulling or pushing them).

11. (A) We **covered a lot of ground** at the meeting.
    (B) I'd like to **return** to the point I was making earlier.
    (C) After three hours, we finally **arrived** at a decision.

    Metaphorically, a / an .... is like a journey, with the people who are speaking going from one place to another.

12. (A) We need to address the social **ills** that are at the root of crime.
    (B) The country was **paralyzed** by a series of natural and man-made disasters.
    (C) Drugs such as heroin and cocaine are seen as a **cancer** at the very heart of society.

    Metaphorically, a / an .... is like an illness.

13. (A) The speaker received a very **warm** welcome from the audience.
    (B) We had several good ideas, but they **poured cold water** on all of them.
    (C) I was disappointed because his response was rather **lukewarm**.

    Metaphorically, ... and .... are like heat, and a lack of these is like being cold or wet.

14. (A) The biography mainly dealt with his years **at the top**.
    (B) Many people commented on his rapid **ascent up the ladder**.
    (C) His greed and lack of integrity eventually led to his **downfall**.

    Metaphorically, being .... is like being high up, and .... is like falling or being low down.

Modified words

Exercise 1

Modify (change) each word in **bold** in the sentences by adding a prefix from the box, so that the word is correct in the context of the sentence. Use each prefix once only.

auto	bi	circum	co	inter	micro	mono	over	post	pre	semi
sub	tele	trans	under	uni						

1. Thanks to Internet technology, companies can hold ....**conferences** with their agents and customers around the world without leaving the office.

2. The conference is a ....**annual** event, and usually takes place in March and September.

3. In her new ....**biography**, the travel writer and broadcaster Lucy Apps treats her readers to some fascinating tales about her life on the open road.

4. E-mail and social networking Web sites have ....**formed** the way people communicate.

5. Unfortunately, the project team exceeded its ....**determined** level of spending, and had to borrow more money.

6. Despite being knocked out of the basketball tournament in the ....**-final**, there was a great sense of elation, and the certainty that our team would go all the way the next time.

7. Only a small percentage of students who do a university degree go on to do ....**graduate** studies.

8. People enjoy their jobs much more if they get on with their ....**-workers**.

9. If you knew about all the potentially dangerous ....**-organisms** that live on an average dishcloth, you would probably never use one again!

10. ....**sex** fragrances are believed to be a modern invention, but a century ago all perfumes were for men and women alike, and people just chose the one they liked the most.

11. If you feel that you have received ....**standard** service, you should complain to the manager or most senior employee immediately rather than wait until later.

12. In 1929, the Graf Zeppelin became the first airship to ....**navigate** the world.

13. Astronauts started living on the ....**national** Space Station in 2000.

14. I have two dictionaries: an English-Spanish one, and a ....**lingual** English one.

15. I was an ....**achiever** at school, always getting low grades in tests and poor marks in my homework.

16. The city is so ....**populated** that it is almost impossible to find anywhere to live.

Exercise 2

Now do the same with these. Use the same prefixes from the box in Exercise 1.

1. ....**waves** work by passing electricity through food rather than by heating it.

2. The late twentieth century saw enormous advances in .... **communications**, with the development of the Internet being of particular importance.

3. In 1986, against everybody else's wishes, the ruling government made the ....**lateral** decision to close half the country's coal mines.

4.   In ancient Roman theaters, the audience sat outside in a ....**circle**.

5.   On long-distance flights, the aircraft is flown by ....**pilot** most of the time, with the real pilots only assuming occasional control.

6.   I speak English and French, but my French is quite limited, so unfortunately I wouldn't say I'm ....**lingual**.

7.   There are strict laws against advertising tobacco products, but with a bit of imagination, many of these can be easily ....**vented**.

8.   A lot of the city was destroyed during the war, so during the immediate ....**-war** years, the government embarked on a massive reconstruction program.

9.   I think I passed my exams, but it would be ....**mature** to say that I've done well in all of them.

10.   A third of the children were found to be ....**weight** as a result of a high-fat, high-sugar diet.

11.   It is believed that many people who dislike water have a ....**conscious** fear of drowning.

12.   Most of the schools in my country are ....**educational**, although there are a few boy-only and girl-only institutions.

13.   We ran out of money because we had ....**estimated** how much the trip would cost.

14.   The aviator Charles Lindbergh made the first solo ....**atlantic** flight in 1927.

15.   Part of our course was to study the ....**relationship** between stress and illness, and especially to what extent one resulted in the other.

16.   He knew a lot about his subject, but he spoke in such a dull ....**tone** that his students would often fall asleep.

Exercise 3

Complete these sentence with words from Exercises 1 and 2. In some cases, you will need to change the form and / or function of the word (e.g., from an adjective to a noun).

1.   Professor McGuire tells me that I .... my abilities, and that I'm much better than I think I am.

2.   I enjoyed reading his ...., but I think he made half of it up.

3.   .... babies are extremely vulnerable to disease, so human contact must be kept to a minimum.

4.   .... in major urban centers can lead to riots and demonstrations, especially if living conditions are very poor.

5.   I can't stand my boss, but my .... are OK.

6.   The first .... underwater telephone cable was laid between Scotland and Canada in 1956.

7.   .... the city into a major cultural and artistic center attracted thousands of tourists who would otherwise not have gone there.

8.   When he started his company, he had just one small .... hair salon in the city center.

9.   He felt happy, but .... he knew that he was not really content with life.

10.   The company sends its shareholders a .... report outlining its targets for the next six months.

Numbers and symbols

How do you say the numbers and symbols in **bold** in these sentences?

1.   **2011** was the company's most profitable year since **1998**.

2.   The advantage of Internet banking is that you can check your account **24/7**.

3.   Despite a rigorous advertising campaign, demand has only risen by **0.8**% in the last two months.

4.   We're meeting in his office at **3:45** this afternoon.

5.   Your flight for Zurich leaves at **1800** from Logan International Airport.

6.   I expect to be back in the country on **June 30**.

7.   Our next range of products will be released on **10/3**.

8.   She completed the test in a record **27½** minutes.

9.   **¾** of all our employees think the canteen food could be improved.

10.   The new desk measures exactly **2m** x **1m** x **1m.**

11.   Is this printer really only **$1.99**?

12.   Oh, sorry sir, that's a mistake. The sticker should say **$100.99**.

13.   And that computer doesn't cost **$120.75**. It actually costs **$1,120.75**.

14.   Please quote reference **ACB81 - 25/B**.

15.   Our new telephone number is **020 7921 3567**.

16.   For more information, call **0845 601 5884**.

17.   Alternatively, ring **0800 231415**.

18.   The emergency telephone number in the UK is **999**. In the United States it's **911**. In Australia it's **000**.

19.   To access the information you require, press the **#** key, followed by the **0** key, and finally the ***** key.

20.   He earns a salary of over **$200K** a year! In fact, he's making so much money that he plans to retire in his **mid-50s**.

21.   We have invested over **$6M** in new technology.

22.   The union held a ballot to see if the workers wanted to strike. The result was **2:1** in favor.

23.   My email address is markbarrington**@snailmail.com**.

24.   Hi Todd. **GR8** news on the promotion. I'm really **:-)** for you! **CUL8R** for a celebratory drink?

25.   He drives to work in a big, fuel-guzzling **4x4**.

26.   The Denver Deadbeats won the match against the Washington Washouts by **2:0**. In the match against the Los Angeles Layabouts the following week, they drew **3:3**.

27.   At the last census, the population of the country was **37,762,418**.

28.   It's important to send your **1099** form to the IRS on time.

29.   This book is **©** Rawdon Wyatt.

30.   The 'Ultimafone**®**' has just won a Product of the Year award.

Obligation and option

Complete the sentences with a suitable word from the box. More than one answer is possible in some cases.

alternative   compelled   compulsory   essential   exempt   forced   have   liable   mandatory   must   need   obligation   obliged   optional   require   voluntary

1. A valid passport and visa are .... by all visitors to the country. Unless you have these, you will not be allowed in.

2. Attendance at all classes is .... You may not miss a lesson without prior arrangement with your course leader.

3. Note to new students: all fees .... be paid no later than one week before the commencement of the course. Your place on the course may be forfeited if you fail to satisfy this requirement.

4. Before you make an appointment with the college doctor, you .... to register your name at the clinic, which you will find in the Administrative Block.

5. If you cause any damage to property, whether accidentally or on purpose, you will be held .... for any costs incurred.

6. The college was .... to refund part of its student fees after they announced that several of the course modules would no longer be running.

7. Books, clothes, and food are currently .... from government tax, as they are considered necessities rather than luxuries.

8. .... police security checks are carried out on all students and members of staff who will be working or associating with minors (i.e., those under 18).

9. Entrance to the museum is free, but visitors are asked to make a .... donation of $5.

10. Evening lectures and presentations are ....: it is up to you whether you attend or not.

11. Unless your attendance improves, the college will have no .... but to ask you to leave the course.

12. Manufacturers of packaged foods are .... to list all the ingredients contained clearly on the box or package. This should include any artificial colorings and additives.

13. You are under no .... to work overtime, but we hope that you would be prepared to work late at least once a week.

14. When Professor Ranscombe was accused of making sexist remarks in his lectures, he felt .... to write a public letter of apology to those he had offended.

15. There's no .... to make an appointment to see me. Just turn up at my office anytime after lunch.

16. It is absolutely .... that the two liquids are kept separate, otherwise a chemical reaction could trigger an explosion.

Opinion, attitude, and belief

<u>Exercise 1</u>

Complete the crossword with the correct forms of the words in **bold** in sentences 1 – 20. The first one has been done as an example.

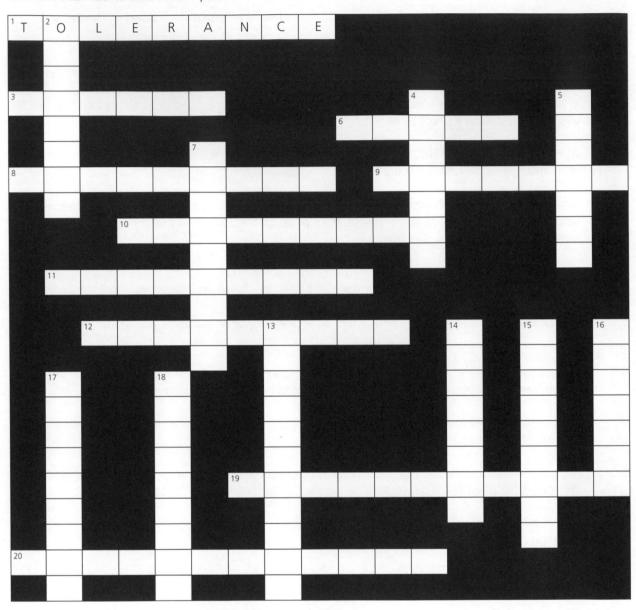

1.   I think that people need to show greater **tolerate** of each other.

2.   Some major companies are **obsession** with secrecy.

3.   I **reckoning** that global warming is having more of an effect than we think.

4.   We strongly **suspicious** that the proposal to develop the computer facilities will be rejected.

5.   Some people are extremely **bigotry**, especially regarding things like race or religion.

6.   I very much **doubtful** that the situation will improve in the near future.

7.   A lot of people are **fanatic** about sport in general and baseball in particular.

8.   He was very hard-working and **dedication** to his research.

9.   In my **opinionated**, people don't take enough exercise.

10. I consider myself to be a **pragmatist** person, and believe that results are more important than theories or ideas.

11. Team members need to be completely **commitment**, and prepared to work for long hours.

12. The current administration is **regardless** foreign debt, especially in developing countries, as a major barrier to global economic development.

13. People often indicate their **disapprove** of something through their body language rather than words.

14. I **maintenance** that many young people would rather work than continue with their studies.

15. As far as I am **concerning**, happiness is more important than money.

16. Unhappy people often have a **cynic** view of life.

17. I take strong **exceptional** to people coming late or canceling appointments at short notice.

18. Many scientists are **convincingly** that human activity is threatening the future of many animal and plant species.

19. My parents are **tradition** people who believe that children should not have too much freedom.

20. He had very **conservatism** views and did not like change of any sort.

Exercise 2
Complete these sentences with the words from Exercise 1. You will either need a word from the sentences or from the completed crossword. In some cases, more than one answer may be possible.

1. People are often .... of strangers, and refuse to trust anyone unless they know them very well.

2. She's very well organized, and always takes a .... approach to problem solving,

3. I'm absolutely .... about keeping fit, and go to the gym at least once a day.

4. I strongly .... of smoking, and refuse to let people smoke in my home.

5. My .... is that people who read a lot are more interesting than people who don't.

6. To succeed in life, you need ambition and ....

7. My father won't .... anyone who questions his decisions.

8. Small farm communities are predominantly .... in their outlook and behavior.

9. Some people .... my ability to succeed, but I am determined to prove they are wrong.

10. A lot of people in my country .... that the current economic crisis will get worse before it gets better.

Complete the definitions with the nouns and adjectives from the box.

agnostic   anarchist   atheist   Democrat   intellectual   moderate open-minded   opinionated   pacifist   Republican   stoical   superstitious tolerant   vegan   vegetarian

1.   Someone who is well educated and interested in art, science, literature, etc., at a high level is a / an
....

2.   Someone who accepts bad things without complaining is ....

3.   Someone who is willing to accept other people's beliefs, way of life, etc., without criticizing them
(even if they disagree with them) is ....

4.   (In the United States) Someone with conservative political views, and who supports the political
party with similar views, is a / an ....

5.   (In the United States) Someone with more liberal political views than the person above, and who
supports the political party with similar views, is a / an ....

6.   Someone who is willing to consider new ideas is ....

7.   Someone who believes that there should be no governments or laws is a / an
....

8.   Someone who believes that violence is wrong and refuses to fight in or support wars is a / an
....

9.   Someone who chooses not to eat meat or fish is a ....

10.   Someone who chooses not to eat *anything* made from, or produced by, animals, including fish,
eggs, milk, cheese, and honey is a / an ....

11.   Someone who believes in the power of magic or luck is ....

12.   Someone who does not believe in God is a / an ....

13.   Someone who believes that it is not possible to know whether God exists or not is
....

14.   Someone whose opinions and actions are reasonable and not extreme, especially in politics, is a / an
....

15.   Someone who has very strong opinions that they refuse to change, even when they are clearly
unreasonable, is ....

Opposites 1: Verbs

Exercise 1

Replace the verbs in **bold** in the sentences with a verb from the box which has an opposite meaning in the same context. In many cases you will need to change the form of the word (for example, to its past simple form). The first one has been done as an example.

abandon	abolish	attack	conceal	demolish	deny	deteriorate
exaggerate	extend	fall	gain	hire	ignore	lend	loosen	lower
postpone	refuse	~~reject~~	replenish	retreat	reward	set	simplify
succeed	withdraw					

1.   When our trip was canceled, we **accepted** the travel company's offer of a partial refund. _...rejected..._
2.   She **admitted** that she had borrowed my camera without asking me.
     ....
3.   Aerial footage shows how rapidly the floods are **advancing**. ....
4.   They **agreed** to meet to discuss the future of the organization. ....
5.   The Senator **defended** his opponent's policies in a televised speech. ....
6.   The apartment blocks they **built** were the ugliest in the city. ....
7.   He **complicated** matters by rewriting the original proposal. ....
8.   When the money ran out, they had to decide whether or not to **continue** their research.
     ....
9.   He **deposited** $10,000 – half his college fees for the forthcoming year.
     ....
10. Relations between the two countries have **improved** considerably in the last year.
     ....
11. Everyone **acknowledged** all the hard work I had done. ....
12. In my opinion, **punishing** young children for their behavior is wrong. ....
13. He **raised** the overall standards of the company within two months of his appointment.
     ....
14. As soon as the sun starts to **rise**, animals appear at the watering hole. ....
15. Prices **rose** sharply in the first three months of the financial year. ....
16. Before you do anything else, make sure you **tighten** the knots in the rope.
     ....
17. To everyone's surprise, she **failed**. ....
18. Tomorrow's meeting has been **brought forward**. ....
19. The management said that they would be happy to **borrow** the money.
     ....
20. Several flaws in the design of the new model were **revealed**. ....
21. The course has been **shortened** to 12 weeks. ....
22. I don't want to **underestimate** his role in the club. ....
23. Fuel supplies have been **exhausted**. ....
24. Despite having a bigger and cheaper choice of healthy foods, many Americans have **lost** a lot of weight. ....
25. Following the revolution, the monarchy was **restored**. ....
26. The company started seeing some success once they **dismissed** several employees.
     ....

Exercise 2

Some verbs can be made into their opposite form, or otherwise modified, by the addition of the prefixes *dis-*, *im-*, *mis-*, or *un-*.

In each of the sentences below, change the verb in **bold** into its opposite form using one of the prefixes above. In most cases, you should also need to change the end of the verb (by adding *-s*, *-ed*, *-ing*, etc., and in some cases by also removing a letter). Then use your answers to complete the crossword on the next page. The first one has been done as an example.

Across (⇨)

2. The press have once again **quote** the President: he said that women were 'America's hope for the future', and not 'America's hopeless future'.

3. The National Patients' Association is calling on Senators around the country to make doctors legally responsible for **diagnose** an illness.

6. Despite recent rumors in the press, Kaput Computers is pleased to announce that it will *not* be **continue** its popular range of discounted computers for students.

8. The press deliberately tried to **represent** our college, wrongly suggesting that we only recruit students whose parents make large financial donations to the college.

10. Once the boxes have been **load** from the truck, they are placed in a dark, dry room.

12. If any student **agree** with the new regulations, he or she should put their concerns in a letter to the Course Director.

13. If any student **use** the college computers (e.g., for accessing undesirable Web sites), they will be instantly suspended.

14. In his new book *Stars in my Eyes*, astronomer Harvey Weiss claims to **lock** the secrets of the universe.

16. As the full extent of the disaster **fold**, the government decided to take drastic action.

20. Employers have every right to **trust** interview candidates who are not able to provide adequate references or show proof of their qualifications.

22. The college principal **approve** of students smoking on the premises.

23. He **obey** the rules, and got into trouble as a result.

Down (⬇)

1. We completely **judge** the time we had for the project, and unfortunately we were unable to finish on time.

2. When one group of people **understand** another, usually as a result of linguistic or cultural differences, physical conflict is often the result.

4. Before **connect** the copier from the power supply, make sure it is switched off.

5. Students who are caught cheating will be immediately **qualify**.

7. Your lack of progress on this course has **please** your tutor, and in view of this he plans report you to the Principal.

9. I accidentally **calculate** the amount we needed to spend on fees and accommodation.

11. It is a sad fact of college life that unless some students are properly supervised, they will take every opportunity to **behave**.

15. We claimed $20,000 for fire damage, but the claim was **allow** because we hadn't observed proper safety procedures.

17. We regret that our trust in you was sadly **place**, and therefore we will not be dealing with you in the future.

18. A recent investigation has **cover** several cases of unauthorized Internet use in the library.

19. The huge increase in exports recently has **prove** the argument that the world has stopped buying American goods.

21. Unfortunately, but not surprisingly, many of our students **like** the increased workload this semester.

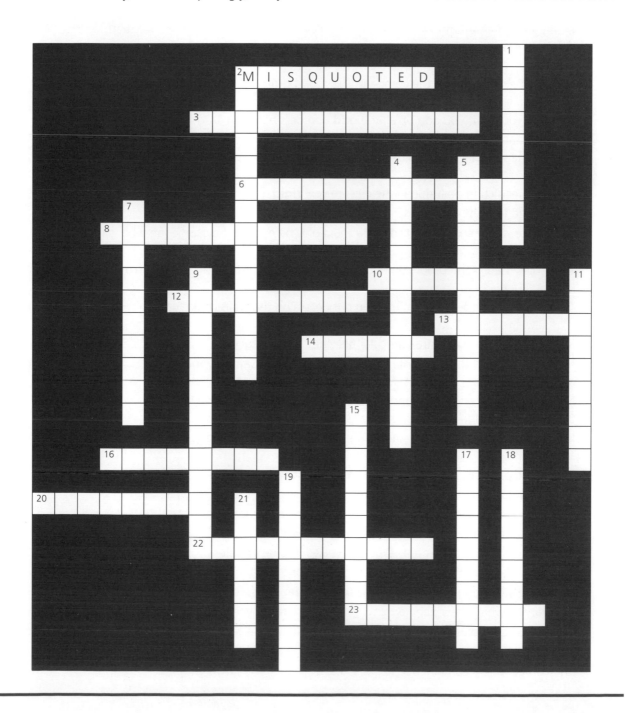

Opposites 2: Adjectives

<u>Exercise 1</u>

Replace the adjectives in **bold** in sentences 1 – 28 with a word from the box which has an opposite meaning in the same context. The first one has been done as an example

approximate	archaic	artificial	~~clear~~	commonplace	compulsory
considerable	crude	delicate	detrimental	dim	easy	even	feasible
flexible	graceful	innocent	intricate	negligible	problematic	scarce
smooth	reluctant	spontaneous	tedious	vibrant	worthless	worthwhile

1.   The terms and conditions of the contract are very **ambiguous**. ....*clear*...........
2.   According to the people who worked with him, he was a very **awkward** person to deal with. ....
3.   I had never seen a dancer who was so **clumsy**. ....
4.   The changes he made were **beneficial** to the organization as a whole. ....
5.   We need **exact** figures before we decide if we can go ahead with the project. ....
6.   Following a lengthy trial, the company was found **guilty** of negligence. ....
7.   What do you get if you add up all the **odd** numbers between 1 and 100? ....
8.   Despite the weather, supplies of food after the harvest were **plentiful**. ....
9.   The laws restricting pollution in the city are very **rigid**. ....
10. I've noticed a **slight** difference in his attitude these last few weeks. ....
11. The device is very **sophisticated** and should only be operated by someone who is familiar with it. ....
12. The spices used in the production of some international dishes have a very **strong** flavor. ....
13. The **bright** light from the torch picked out details on the walls of the cave. ....
14. Student attendance at extra-curricular activities is **voluntary**. ....
15. Most students say they are **willing** to attend classes on Saturday morning. ....
16. Newspapers are saying a lot about the country's **modern** licensing laws. ....
17. Many students believe that doing voluntary work for charities is a **pointless** cause. ....
18. The country displayed all the features of a **stagnant** economy. ....
19. Her lectures are extremely **interesting**. ....
20. **Planned** demonstrations and strikes took place all over the city. ....
21. The plans they presented were **simple** and well written. ....
22. A close study of the painting by experts revealed it to be **priceless**. ....
23. The new rules had a **profound** impact on everyone's behavior. ....
24. What you are asking me to do is quite **impossible**. ....
25. Contrary to what many people think, this is a very **rare** event. ....
26. Organizing a fundraising event can be surprisingly **simple**. ....
27. From a distance, the surface of the planet appears to be very **rough**. ....
28. The confectionery contained several flavors, all of them **natural**. ....

Exercise 2

A lot of adjectives can be made into their opposite form by adding a *prefix* (*un-*, *in-*, *dis-*, *il-*, etc.) to the beginning of the word.

Task 1: Add the prefixes in the first box to the words in the second box to make opposites. The first one has been done for you.

dis- il- im- in- ir- un-

.*un*acceptable .....accurate .....adequate .....advantaged .....agreeable

.....attractive .....authorized .....avoidable .....believable .....certain

.....comfortable .....competent .....complete .....conscious .....contented

.....convincing .....correct .....curable .....even .....fair .....fashionable

.....honest .....inclined .....legal .....limited .....literate .....logical

.....married .....mature .....moral .....mortal .....obedient

.....organized .....patient .....perfect .....personal .....possible

.....proper .....pure .....qualified .....rational .....regular

.....relevant .....replaceable .....resistible .....resolute .....responsible

.....satisfactory .....satisfied .....sufficient .....welcome

Task 2: Without looking at your answers to Task 1, look at the following sentences and paragraphs. In each one there is *one* word in **bold** which has been given the <u>wrong prefix</u>. Decide which word is wrong and correct it.

1. He is a very **disagreeable** man and he makes visitors feel very **unwelcome**, but the management think he's **irreplaceable** and are **uninclined** to fire him.

2. Insider dealing is not only **immoral** and **inhonest**, but also **illegal**: companies are legally bound to take the strongest possible action against such **unacceptable** behavior by their employees.

3. It is an **unavoidable** fact, but in a competitive job market, those who are **unqualified** or who have **imsufficient** work experience will find themselves seriously **disadvantaged**.

4. She was described by her boss as being **unresponsible**, **incompetent,** and **immature**, which she considered extremely **unfair**.

5. In return for an increased investment, the company offered **unlimited** returns for their investors. While many found such an offer **irresistible**, some thought the promises were **inconvincing** and were **uncomfortable** about parting with so much money.

6. He had clearly given his presentation **disadequate** preparation, and many in the audience challenged the points he made, saying they were **inaccurate** and **illogical**. Despite this, he remained **irresolute** in his views, although the only person he managed to convince was himself.

Phrasal verbs 1

Phrasal verbs are very common in English, and should be learnt like any other item of English vocabulary. In the TOEFL®, they are tested in the Listening Comprehension section, and appear frequently in other parts of the test.

<u>Exercise 1</u>

In the following sentences, choose the correct verb in **bold** to complete the phrasal verb in *italics*. The meaning of each phrasal verb you need is given in brackets at the end of each sentence.

1.   Some parents are criticized for the way they **bring / make / throw** *up* their children. (*to raise children*)

2.   They refused to **move / face / come** *up to* their responsibilities, with disastrous consequences. (*to accept an unpleasant state of affairs, and try to deal with it*)

3.   The President decided to **shout / cry / call** *off* his visit to Europe. (*to not to go ahead with a plan*)

4.   It is only at election time that Senators **add / count / read** *on* support from their constituents. (*to rely / depend on other people*)

5.   Many developing countries are failing to **run / chase / catch** *up with* their more developed neighbors. (*to get to the same level*)

6.   It can take months or even years for political scandals to **die / cut / fall** *down*. (*to become less strong*)

7.   An alarming number of students **jump / drop / fall** *out of* school early every year. (*to leave a race, a competition, a course of study, etc., early or before you have finished*)

8.   Major international companies can't **carry / cut / figure** *out* the popularity of the anti-capitalist movement. (*informal: to find it hard to understand*)

9.   The committee members **dropped / made / fell** *out* over plans for the new health center. (*to argue*)

10.   If they examined the issues more closely, they would **search / look / find** *out* the reasons. (*to discover*)

11.   As we **grow / stand / look** *up* our priorities change. (*to change from being children to being adults*)

12.   Salaries very rarely **catch / keep / work** *up with* the cost of living. (*to rise at the same speed as something else*)

13.   The problem with the survey is that it **leaves / keeps / throws** *out* the real reasons for current demographic shifts. (*to not include*)

14.   The journalist **showed / pointed / spoke** *out* the mistakes made by the agency over the last few years. (*to show*)

15.   Before you write your essay, you should **search / hunt / look** *into* the Party's history. (*to research*)

16.   Nobody at the meeting **carried / brought / moved** *up* the subject of paid leave. (*to start discussing a subject*)

17.   Once people **lose / jump / fall** *behind* with their mortgage payments, they come under extreme financial pressure from their bank. (*to fail to do something or pay something at the time that you should*)

18.   The first step to a healthier lifestyle is to **cut / slice / chop** *down* on the amount of saturated fats you eat. (*to start doing less of something, usually because it is bad for you*)

Exercise 2

Now do the same with these. In one of the sentences, all three verbs are possible without a change in meaning.

1. During the early 2000s, a lot of state-run hospitals were **controlled** / **taken** / **acquired** over by private trusts. (*to start to do something in place of someone else*)

2. In my last essay, I tried to **argue** / **place** / **put** forward the arguments in favor of global capitalism. (*to suggest or state the case for something*)

3. Despite the seriousness of the illness, he managed to **carry** / **pull** / **take** through. (*to recover from a serious illness or accident*)

4. A lot of restrictions on imports have been **done** / **gone** / **put** away with. (*to get rid of something*)

5. If you have a complaint, put it in writing and ask the company to **investigate** / **look** / **see** into it for you. (*to try to discover the facts about something such as a problem*)

6. It is very important to **carry** / **work** / **do** out my instructions carefully. (*to do something that you have been told to do, often in a particular way*)

7. Many employees **went** / **kept** / **carried** on working despite pressure from the unions. (*to continue*)

8. The drug's effects are very powerful, but they begin to **wear** / **come** / **fall** off after a few hours. (*to gradually disappear or become less intense*)

9. The meeting will be canceled if not enough people **arrive** / **move** / **turn** up. (*to come somewhere, often unexpectedly*)

10. At first, sales of the product were slow, but they **kicked** / **hit** / **picked** up when people realized how useful it was. (*to slowly improve*)

11. I have **given** / **put** / **moved** across several suggestions, but so far they have all been ignored. (*to explain an idea, often in a way that is easy for people to understand*)

12. I **came** / **ran** / **moved** into Laura outside the theater last week. (*to meet someone by chance*)

13. This course has **set** / **moved** / **put** me back by about $2,000. (*informal: to cost someone a particular amount of money, especially a large amount*)

14. When I **look** / **consider** / **move** back on my childhood, I remember the many sacrifices my parents made for me. (*think about something that happened in the past*)

15. We were all disappointed with the way things **turned** / **came** / **changed** out. (*to develop in a particular way or have a particular result*)

16. The exhibition was so popular that a lot of visitors had to be **pushed** / **turned** / **thrown** away. (*to be not allowed to enter a building*)

17. The total cost of the project **makes** / **moves** / **works** out to about $250,000. (*to add up to a particular amount*)

18. The telephone service is rather unreliable, and it's quite common to be **cut** / **shut** / **run** off in the middle of a conversation. (*to be disconnected while talking on the telephone*)

Phrasal verbs 2

Exercise 1

The words in **bold** can be preceded by *come, get, give, go,* or *look* to make a phrasal verb. Complete each sentence with one of these words. In some cases, more than one answer is possible. Make sure you use the correct form of the verb in each one. The phrasal verb is explained in brackets at the end of each sentence.

1.   In rural districts, it can be difficult to .... **by** without a car. (*to work and operate efficiently*)

2.   I'd like you to .... **over** these figures and tell me if you think the project is possible. (*to check something carefully*)

3.   Large industries can no longer .... **away with** dumping industrial waste in rivers. (*to avoid being punished for doing something wrong or illegal*)

4.   Developed countries are usually able to .... **through** a period of recession by drawing on financial reserves. (*to manage to deal with a difficult situation until it is over*)

5.   People who have to .... **after** elderly relatives or other dependents should receive financial support. (*to take care of someone or something and make certain they have everything they need*)

6.   We decided to .... **through** with our plans as soon as we had sufficient capital. (*to do something you have planned or agreed to do, especially after not being sure you wanted to do it*)

7.   It can be very difficult to .... **down to** studying for exams when the weather is nice. (*to start doing something seriously or with a lot of effort*)

8.   Lights .... **out** across the country as power workers went on strike. (*to stop burning or shining*)

9.   The committee were asked to .... **into** the latest crime statistics and try to establish a pattern. (*to try to discover the facts about something such as a problem or crime*)

10.   After years of decline, government investment is revitalizing the area, and things are beginning to .... **up**. (*to get better, or appear to get better*)

11.   Scientists .... **across** the cure by accident, while studying the health benefits of a rare species of plant. (*to find something by chance*)

12.   Very few students .... **forward to** their end-of-semester exams. (*to feel happy and excited about something that is going to happen*)

13.   Generally, people are reluctant to break unpopular rules, but will try to .... **around** them somehow. (*to find a way of dealing with a problem or avoiding it*)

14.   The first step to a healthier lifestyle is to .... **up** smoking. (*to stop doing something you do regularly*)

15.   The governor .... **up against** a lot of opposition from locals when she proposed building a jail near the city limits. (*to have to deal with something difficult or unpleasant*)

16.   Even if you fail the first time, you should .... **on** trying. (*to continue doing something*)

17.   The anti-smoking message is finally .... **through to** people. (*to make someone understand what you are trying to say*)

18.   As ticket prices .... **up**, fewer people go to the theater and prefer to stay at home with a DVD instead. (*to increase in price*)

Exercise 2
Now do the same with these.

1. Doctors realized there was going to be a problem when several people in the same village .... **down with** suspected food poisoning. (*to become ill with a particular disease*)

2. People often .... **up** the idea of starting their own company when they realize the risks that are involved. (*to no longer want to do something*)

3. Before entering into an agreement, it is essential to .... **over** the details very carefully. (*to check something carefully*)

4. People who live in close proximity to one another must learn to .... **on with** their neighbors. (*to try to like someone and be friendly to them*)

5. It was only after he .... **into** his inheritance after his father died that he was able to expand the company. (*to receive money or property when someone dies*)

6. Sometimes it can take me a while to .... **round to** doing important tasks. (*to do something after you have intended to do it for some time*)

7. New legislation lays down strict penalties for vehicles which .... **off** excess exhaust. (*to produce a gas or smell*)

8. People who want to know how to .... **about** starting their own company should talk to a trained adviser. (*to start dealing with a situation, problem, job, etc., in a particular way*)

9. When supply of a particular good exceeds demand, it is common for the price to .... **down**. (*to become cheaper*)

10. Nothing .... **of** the company's plans to develop solar-powered vehicles. (*to be the result of something*)

11. The final bill for the project will .... **to** almost $10 million. (*to reach a particular total when everything is added together*)

12. For most poor people, ... **out of** the cycle of poverty can be next to impossible. (*to avoid or escape from an unpleasant situation*)

13. In any dispute with an insurance company, it is usually the consumer who .... **off** the worst. (*to achieve a particular result in an activity, especially a competition, fight, or argument*)

14. It took a long time for the country to .... **over** the effects of the disaster. (*to recover from something*)

15. The threat of severe punishment means that many criminals refuse to .... themselves **up** to the police. (*to surrender to someone in a position of authority, especially to the police*)

16. Some people tend to .... **down on** others who are less fortunate purely because of their financial situation. (*to think that you are better or more important than someone else*)

17. The government had decided to stand firm on their decision, but under pressure from protesters, they decided to .... **in** and reduce tax on gasoline. (*to stop competing or arguing and accept that you cannot win*)

18. By the time the message .... **through**, it was too late to evacuate the residents. (*to be connected to someone by telephone, email, text message, etc.*)

Phrasal verbs 3

- The verbs and particles in the two boxes below can be combined to make phrasal verbs, which can then be used to complete the sentences underneath.

- Decide which phrasal verbs go into each sentence, and write the answers in the crossword grid, which you will find on page 44. In many cases, you will need to change the form of the verb (e.g., past or present participle, third person 's', etc.). The meaning of each phrasal verb is in *italics* at the end of each sentence. The first one has been done as an example

- Don't forget that some phrasal verbs need *two* particles.

- Do <u>not</u> put a gap between the verb and the particle(s) in the crossword grid.

add	break	bring	engage
factor	go	hand	hold	make
opt	pick	put	run	set
shut	stem	take	talk	turn

about	after	against	apart
aside	down	for	from	in
into	of	off	on	out
round	to	up	with

Clues across (➔)

1. Housing in some cities is so expensive that some people cannot even afford to
    ....*put down*........................ the deposit that is required. (*to make a deposit*)

5. They were reluctant to make changes, but we managed to .... them
    .... (*to persuade somebody*)

6. Children often .... one of their parents, either in their mannerisms or
    in the way they look. (*to resemble*)

7. After .... a few unexpected difficulties, they decided to scrap the
    project. (*to stop because something is in the way*) (*3 words*)

9. When Mr and Mrs Johnson were unable to pay the rent on time, their landlord threatened to
    .... them .... onto the street.
    (*to force someone to leave*)

10. When I was at school, some teachers unfairly .... children who
    eschewed sport for more creative interests and pastimes. (*to choose someone to attack or criticize*)

11. Although many companies offer their employees a pension scheme, many decide to
    .... of the program and make their own arrangements. (*to decide not
    to take part in something*)

16. A lot of applicants expressed an interest in the job, but only a handful ....
    for the interview. (*to arrive for a meeting, appointment, etc.*)

19. Air pollution can .... asthma and other chest diseases in those most
    vulnerable. (*to start*)

20. People who use credit cards unwisely can easily .... debts of
    thousands of dollars every month. (*to make debts go up quickly*)

22. Parents often struggle to .... enough money to pay for their children's
    education. (*to keep or save something from a larger amount in order to use it later for a particular purpose*)

24. The two men didn't .... each other at first, but over the next year
    they became the best of friends. (*to begin to like someone or something*)

28. One of the best ways to get fit is to .... a sport or activity. (*to start
    doing something regularly as a habit*)

30. The plans were .... while we waited for a decision from the
    management. (*to cause a delay or make someone late*)

32.   The two sides are currently .... talks which they hope will end the dispute. (*to take part in a particular activity, especially something that takes a lot of time and effort*)

36.   Her discovery .... a chain of events that surprised everyone involved. (*to cause a situation or a series of events to happen*)

37.   After .... expenditure and inflation, profits were very low. (*to include a particular amount when you calculate something*)

38.   Our money is .... quickly, and if we don't act soon, it will be too late. (*to use all of something and not have any left*)

39.   Some students can be very creative with the reasons they give for not .... their assignments on time. (*to give something to a person in authority*)

Clues down (⬇)

1.   It's often a good idea to .... some money for a 'rainy day'. (*to save money*)

2.   Technology is moving at such a fast pace it is no longer possible to .... all the latest developments. (*to understand or assimilate information*)

3.   Radical measures introduced by the college authorities did not .... a genuine reform of the system. (*to combine to produce a particular result or effect*) (*3 words*)

4.   Nobody was .... by the government's false figures on unemployment. (*to be fooled or tricked*)

6.   He .... the job that was offered to him, even though he was desperate for the money. (*to refuse something which is offered*)

8.   Most people will .... a stressful job if the money is good enough. (*to tolerate something which is not very pleasant*) (*3 words*)

12.   Once the equipment has been ...., it is surprisingly difficult to put it back together again. (*to separate an object into pieces*)

13.   The revolution was a long, bitter affair which .... neighbor .... neighbor. (*to cause two people or groups to fight each other, even though they were in a friendly relationship before*)

14.   Doctors and medical experts were unable to .... why some people survived the virus and others didn't. (*to understand or know the reason for something*)

15.   Nobody believed the Senator's explanation for a moment. They all knew he had .... it .... (*to invent an explanation for something*)

17.   At the age of 38 he .... the post of President, but lacked sufficient experience to be taken seriously. (*to apply for a job in politics, competing against other people for the same job*)

18.   Despite massive promotion by the tourist board, it took a long time for tourism to .... again after the terrorist attacks. (*to improve, to get better*)

21.   Nothing can .... the damage caused as a result of his actions. (*to take the place of something that has been lost or damaged, or to compensate for something bad that has happened*) (*3 words*)

23.   The group plans to .... an import business by the end of the year. (*to start something such as a business or organization*)

25.   The results of new rules will start to .... next month, by which time we should all have familiarized ourselves with the system. (*informal: to start to have an effect*)

26.   His popularity .... the fact that he was born in the area. (*to be caused by something*)

27.   The project should succeed, unless someone decides to .... at the last minute. (*to stop being involved in an activity, event or situation*)

29. For years women were .... the political process. (*not allowed to do something or not allowed to be involved in something*) (*3 words*)

31. Major spending is required to .... substantial improvement in housing. (*to make something happen, especially to cause changes in a situation*)

33. After several guests had .... food poisoning, public health inspectors were called to the hotel. (*to become ill with a particular illness*) (*3 words*)

34. It has always been my ambition to .... show business. (*to start to have success in your career or an area of activity*)

35. At the auction, the painting .... for an incredible $60 million. (*to be sold for a particular amount of money*)

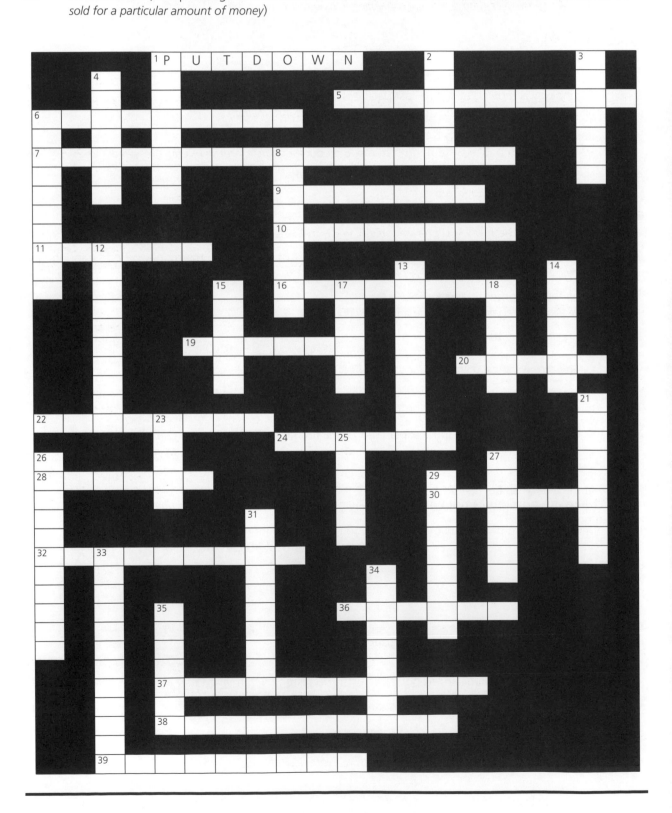

Presenting an argument

Look at the writing task in the box and the sample answer which follows it. <u>Underline</u> the most appropriate words and phrases in **bold** in the answer. In several cases, both options are possible. The first one has been done for you.

> *Some say that young people should take a break between school and college or university to go traveling and learn more about the world. Others say that it is better for them to go straight to college or university when they finish school, and then go traveling when they have finished their studies.*
>
> What do you think? Use specific reasons and examples to support your answer.

These days, it is very common for young people to take time off studying between school and college. Many of them go traveling, and spend a year or longer visiting interesting and exotic places. (1) **But / <u>However</u>**, is it better to do this, or to continue studying without a break?

(2) **First of all / Firstly**, there are several benefits to taking time off to travel. (3) **As well as / In addition to** meeting lots of interesting people, you can also experience cultures that are very different from your own. (4) **I believe / I think** that first-hand knowledge and experience of the world around you early in life are useful things to have. (5) **Moreover / Furthermore**, you learn to look after yourself in different and often difficult situations. (6) **Although / While** few people have serious problems when they travel, you will occasionally encounter situations where you need to think and act quickly without having friends or family to turn to. Unfortunately, traveling has its disadvantages (7) **also / as well**, such as homesickness and culture shock. (8) **Despite / Nevertheless**, these inconveniences are an inevitable part of traveling and are greatly outweighed by the advantages.

(9) **The most important reason / The main reason** for going straight to university after school is the fact that the sooner you get qualifications, the quicker you can get a job and start earning. (10) **As far as I am concerned / For me**, starting work and making money is one of the most important things in life. I am not alone in this opinion. (11) **Many consider / Many say** a sound career with a good salary to be one of life's most important goals. (12) **Second / Secondly**, if you go straight to university, you learn so many things that will help you in your future life. (13) **Eventually / Finally**, going straight to university from school means that you maintain a momentum that you might lose if you go traveling. (14) **I mean / In other words**, you remain focused on studying.

(15) **In conclusion / To summarize**, I would say that spending a year traveling between leaving school and starting university has its advantages and disadvantages. (16) **On the one hand / To begin**, you are seeing something of the world. (17) **After that / On the other hand**, you are delaying your education and career. (18) **In my opinion / I opinion that**, it is better to carry on with your studies, and leave the traveling until later.

Using the key words and expressions in **bold** from Exercise 1, present an argument for <u>one</u> of the following issues, or choose one of the essays from the Topics section of the book:

1.   A government's main priority is to provide education for its people.

2.   The only way to save the environment is for governments to impose strict quotas on the energy we use (for example, by restricting car ownership, limiting the water we use).

3.   Satisfaction in your job is more important than the money you earn.

4.   Living in a town or city is better than living in the countryside.

Pronouns and determiners

<u>Exercise 1</u>

Complete these sentences with an appropriate pronoun or determiner from the box. You will need to use some of the words more than once.

herself himself it its itself ourselves that their theirs them themselves there they those which whose yours yourself

1. The team arrived in Cairo, and from .... set out across the desert in a southwesterly direction.

2. Students are allowed to hand in .... assignments a few days late if they ask for permission at least a week in advance.

3. The new laws made .... easier to get a passport and travel abroad.

4. Someone called for you, but you weren't here, so I told .... you would call when you got back.

5. Many playwrights like to act in the plays they have written. Shakespeare .... appeared in productions of his own works.

6. Most students spend more time on their assignments than .... should.

7. Why did you say that I've missed lots of lessons this semester? Where did you get .... idea? I haven't missed a single one.

8. Greek and Latin are languages from .... many English words have been taken or adapted.

9. This coffee must be ...., not mine . It's got cream in, and I never take cream.

10. You need to ask .... just one question: do I want to be successful, or don't I?

11. The drug works in small quantities, but .... efficacy is reduced if used too much and too often.

12. .... comes a time in everyone's life when a big decision has to be taken.

13. Nuclear energy is far less damaging to the environment than .... produced from fossil fuels, but requires far higher standards of safety to be applied.

14. The authors admitted using material from other books, but we had to give .... credit for their ability to make an otherwise boring subject lively and interesting.

15. A skilled workforce is essential, ... is why regular training programs are so important.

16. The young chick relies on the adult bird for food, and it will be several weeks before it can feed ....

17. The vehicle has a small electric motor, from which .... can get enough power to move without the need for turning the engine on.

18. We should give everyone a chance to say what .... think.

19. Research in the 1960s often took a lot of time and patience, as there was no Internet in .... days.

20. The house stood by .... on a small island, cut off from the outside world by a treacherous reef.

21. When Alice first left home, she found it a challenge looking after ....

22. Her latest book is one .... every teenager will enjoy.

23. Help was offered in the first instance to families .... homes had been destroyed in the earthquake.

24. We need to prepare .... for the struggle that we are about to face.

25. AZB Ltd claimed that the invention was legally .... , and sued their competitor for breaching their design copyright.

Exercise 2

Complete these sentences without looking at the word box in Exercise 1. Then write the letters indicated (e.g., *third letter*, *last letter*, etc.) in the table at the bottom of the page to reveal another determiner.

1. The voice at the end of the phone was .... of a young man. (*First or last letter*)

2. Humphrey Bogart's most famous film was probably *Casablanca*, ... was made in 1942. (*Second or last letter*)

3. The company was forced to cut prices and lay off staff, but the problems didn't end .... (*Third or last letter*)

4. Fees must be paid in full before the course begins. Alternatively, you can pay .... in six monthly instalments through the first semester. (*Last letter*)

5. Prices in New York are roughly 30% cheaper than .... in London. (*Fourth letter*)

6. Newspapers are frequently criticized for invading the privacy of famous people, but on the whole .... tend to ignore it. (*Third letter*)

7. The software has a few glitches, but the real problem lies in the computer, and not in the software .... (*Fifth letter*)

8. Nobody's going to help us. We'll have to do it .... (*Seventh letter*)

9. People who adopt children tend to be people who have no children of .... own but who desperately want some. (*Third letter*)

10. Those who want to see Las Vegas and sample all of .... attractions are going to need a lot of money. (*Last letter*)

1	2	3	4	5	6	7	8	9	10

Use this word in a sentence of your own:

....

....

Similar meanings: Adjectives 1

Here is a crossword with a difference. The words, which are all adjectives, are already in the grid, but some of the letters have been removed. With the help of a dictionary, try to fill in the missing letters. The more letters you fill in, the easier it becomes to complete the grid.

When you have done this, match the adjectives in the grid with a word or expression with a similar meaning which you will find in **bold** on the next page. The first one has been done for you (and the word has been completed and shaded in the crossword grid).

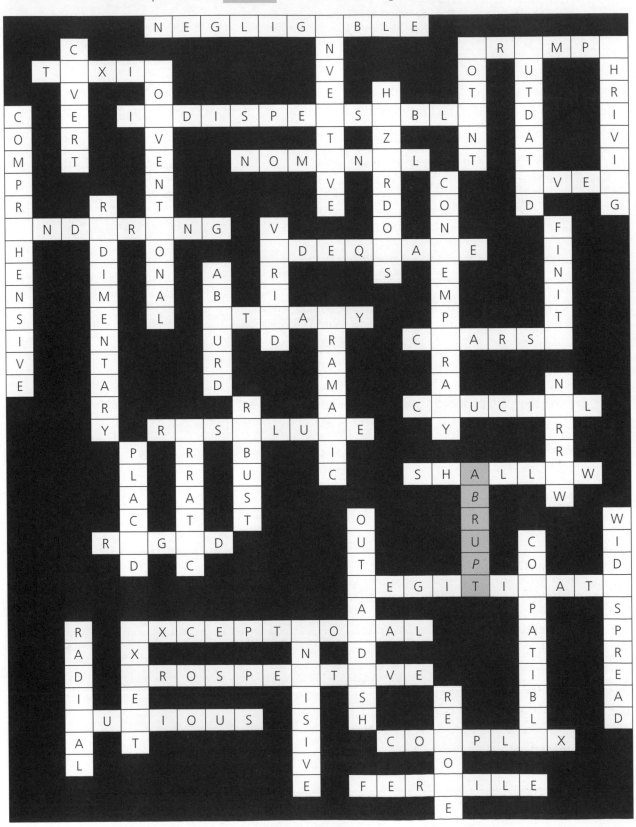

1. A **rude** reply. .... *abrupt* ....
2. A **strong and successful** economy. ....
3. **Basic** facilities. ....
4. A **small** charge for services. ....
5. **Traditional** medicine. ....
6. An **inquisitive** student. ....
7. **Specialist** knowledge. ....
8. An **isolated** village. ....
9. A **ridiculous** idea. ....
10. **Suitable** computer software. ....
11. A **valid** reason for doing something. ....
12. **Strict** economic controls. ....
13. A **calm, peaceful** sea. ....
14. A **small** margin of opportunity. ....
15. A **secret** operation. ....
16. An **insignificant** amount of money ....
17. **Dangerous** chemicals. ....
18. An exhibition of **modern** art. ....
19. **Lasting** appeal. ....
20. **Extremely unusual** circumstances. ....
21. **Very strange or unusual** behavior. ....
22. A **punctual** start to a meeting. ....
23. **Old-fashioned** ideas. ....
24. A **potential or likely** candidate for a job. ....
25. A **thorough** investigation. ....
26. **Enough** information. ....
27. **Slow but steady** progress. ....
28. A **sudden, sharp** rise in prices. ....
29. A **flourishing** community. ....
30. **Difficult and detailed** instructions. ....
31. A **creative** director. ....
32. A **powerful** drug. ....
33. **Extreme** measures to prevent or achieve something. ....
34. A **superficial** person. ....
35. An **unpredictable** sequence of events. ....
36. **Rich** agricultural soil. ....
37. A **level** surface. ....
38. **Very important** information (2 possible words). ....
39. A **diverse** program of events. ....
40. **Essential** raw materials (2 possible words). ....
41. **Poisonous** gases. ....
42. **Clear and direct** comments. ....
43. **Limited** natural resources. ....
44. **Extensive** unemployment. ....
45. A **determined** student. ....
46. **Rough** material. ....

Similar meanings: Adjectives 2

Look at sentences 1 – 14 and choose a word from the box that has a similar meaning to the words and phrases in **bold**. Write these words in the grid below. The first one has been done as an example.

If you do it correctly, you will reveal a word in the shaded vertical strip that is a synonym of the word '*typical*' in this sentence:

*The strong sense of community is **typical** of an area where people feel they are an underclass who must struggle to survive.*

abundant archaic chaotic concise credible evident handsome
industrious integral rampant risky scrupulous tedious tenacious

1. His instructions were very **brief and clear**.

2. The Chrysler Building is one of New York's most **attractive** skyscrapers.

3. Latin is considered by many to be an **outdated** language, despite the fact that many words from the language are still in use today.

4. From a financial point of view it was a very **dangerous** plan.

5. There are **plenty of** opportunities for promotion if you are prepared to work hard.

6. The conference was really **disorganized** and a complete waste of time.

7. His lectures are **boring** and I never seem to learn anything useful or interesting.

8. It was **obvious** that the President had been told what to say by his advisers.

9. **Uncontrolled** corruption and abuse of power by officials eventually prompted new anti-corruption laws.

10. The setting of the scene in chapter one of the book is **essential** to the plot.

11. He gained a reputation as an **honest and fair** dealer, and therefore won the respect of his customers.

12. He was a **resilient** man who believed in fighting for his principles.

13. She was a serious, **hardworking** student who achieved excellent grades.

14. The story seemed **believable** at first, but a bit of research revealed some startling irregularities.

	First letter	Rest of word
1	c	*oncise*
2		
3		
4		
5		
6		
7		
8		
9		
10		
11		
12		
13		
14		

Similar meanings: Nouns

<u>Exercise 1</u>

The sentences below can either be completed with a word from box A *or* a word with a similar meaning from box B. Identify <u>both</u> the words that could be used. The first one has been done for you.

A	B
acclaim accommodation ~~agenda~~ appointment assistance benefits discipline discount drop faults means opposition proof proximity requirements work	advantages closeness decline defects employment evidence help housing meeting method order praise prerequisites resistance reduction ~~schedule~~

1. We have a very busy ....*agenda*.......... / ....*schedule*.......... today, so I suggest we start as soon as possible.

2. The college provides cheap .... / .... for its staff and students.

3. With regard to attendance and punctuality, we need to maintain .... / .... at all times.

4. Thank you for your kind .... / .... : I couldn't have done it without you.

5. There has been a sharp .... / .... in the number of people attending afternoon classes.

6. The early computer program had several .... / .... which need to be sorted out before it could be used.

7. There has been a lot of .... / .... to the new timetable: nobody likes the earlier starts and later finishes to the day.

8. There is no .... / .... to show that standards of living have improved.

9. Students holding a valid student card are eligible for a 10% .... / .... on book prices.

10. The bar is popular with our students because of its .... / .... to the college.

11. I can't see you this afternoon because I have a / an .... / .... with my tutor.

12. The Turkish writer Orhan Pamuk received international .... / .... for his novel *Snow*.

13. At the height of its success, the studio provided .... / .... for over 3,000 people.

14. There are several .... / .... to working from home: you save on travel costs, for one thing.

15. If you want to do a degree in Middle East Studies, a basic knowledge of Arabic is one of the main .... / ....

16. The cheapest .... / .... of traveling around the United States is by Greyhound bus.

Exercise 2

Now do the same with these.

A	B
alterations characteristics choices code cooperation liability magnitude overview priority problems protest questions strategy valid winner zenith	changes collaboration complications demonstration (short) description features good importance options peak plan precedence queries responsibility rules victor

1. The .... / .... against the war spread to most parts of the city by midnight, with at least 50 arrests taking place.

2. The college .... / .... state(s) that students must attend at least 80% of their classes.

3. The college accepts no .... / .... for any damage to vehicles in the car park.

4. There are two .... / .... available to you: work hard on improving your mid-term grades, or consider changing your course.

5. Our latest prospectus provides a / an .... / .... of our courses and a brief history of the university.

6. Nobody understood the .... / .... of the results: it was assumed that everything would stay the same, whereas there were in fact profound changes

7. Thanks to their .... / .... with several affiliated companies, they managed to create a virtual monopoly for their product.

8. I hope you have a .... / .... reason for missing so many of your lessons.

9. The empire reached its .... / .... at the end of the nineteenth century.

10. If you have any .... / ...., please ask a member of staff.

11. A purple rash and a persistent cough is one of the .... / .... of this disease.

12. We had hoped that everything would run smoothly, but unfortunately there have been several .... / ....

13. Before you start studying for the TOEFL®, you should come up with a .... / .... that will help you to make the most of your study time.

14. Safety in the workplace is very important, and should take .... / .... over everything else.

15. Is it necessary to make any .... / .... to the plan, or should we keep it as it is?

16. In the battle of the sexes there can never be a true .... / ....

<u>Exercise 3</u>
Finally, do the same with these.

A	B
achievement advent argument backing category charisma disparity ending inventions notion numbers parts proceeds reviews specialist ultimatum	accomplishment (personal) appeal appearance classification components concentrations difference dispute earnings expert final demand idea innovations support termination write-ups

1.   The book received a lot of good .... / ....
      in the press, and went on to become one of the year's bestsellers.

2.   Before the .... / .... of the home PC
      in the mid-80s, not many people knew how to type.

3.   Unlike his much-loved father, the young leader lacked .... /
      .... and failed to become popular with his people.

4.   The best English dictionaries are those for English-language learners: dictionaries in this
      .... / .... tend to give very clear
      definitions with good examples.

5.   The board ordered the .... / .... of all
      research, with the result that it was another five years before a cure for the illness was found.

6.   Technological .... / .... have changed
      the world in the last 20 years.

7.   Large .... / .... of unskilled,
      unemployed people in certain parts of the country have resulted in a rise in crime and street violence.

8.   I'm not an economics .... / ...., but
      even I know that a drop in unemployment often leads to a rise in inflation.

9.   With .... / .... from her teachers, she
      was able to start an international languages club at the school.

10.   Our new Economics tutor has a strange .... /
      .... that all students are lazy and irresponsible.

11.   You will find the problem easier to solve if you try breaking it down into its separate
      .... / ....

12.   His promotion to Director was a remarkable .... /
      .... for someone so young.

13.   Our head of department gave us a / an .... /
      ....: get down to some serious work or get out.

14.   Despite several changes to the pay structure, there is still a .... /
      .... in pay between graduate trainees and non-graduates.

15.   All .... / .... from the sale of part of
      the grounds will be re-invested in the college.

16.   His irrational behavior eventually led to a serious .... /
      .... with his sponsors.

Similar meanings: Verbs 1

Look at the words and phrases in **bold** in the following sentences, and choose a word from the boxes that has the same or a similar meaning _in the same context_. Write these words after each sentence (the first one has been done for you), then use them to complete the crossword on page 56. You do not need to change any of the word forms.

<u>Across (⇨)</u>

allow	alter	answer	assert	assume	attain	baffle	convey	derive
detect	~~direct~~	enrich	exceed	evolve	refine	relate	remove	resist
reveal	settle	submit	verify					

2. His job is mainly to **control** the activities of everyone in the company with a view to making optimum use of the workforce. ...._direct_...........................

4. We normally **suppose** that most people nowadays have a computer at home. ....

5. Shakespeare said that some people **achieve** greatness, while others have it thrust upon them. ....

6. Did you **notice** a hint of pessimism in her report? ....

11. He was asked to **disclose** government secrets in exchange for money. ....

12. If you want people to take you seriously, you should **state firmly** your reasons for change. ....

13. Antibodies help our bodies to **fight** infection. ....

14. Several attempts were made to **improve** the system. ....

15. Computer software will continue to **develop** in response to users' needs. ....

16. They asked us to **give** our thanks and best wishes to the chairman. ....

19. The two countries have often tried to **resolve** their differences, but to little effect. ....

21. It took him some time to **tell** the story, and it was late when he eventually finished. ....

23. The department was asked to **propose** some ideas for increasing student enrollment. ....

25. A revolutionary new scientific method may soon help to **alter** people's physical appearance without the need for surgery. ....

27. His explanation seemed to **confuse** most people. ....

29. Would you **reply to** his question as briefly as possible. ....

32. The device is able to **confirm** whether a banknote is genuine or a forgery by analyzing the paper and print quality. ....

33. Some plants, such as beans, **benefit** the soil in which they are planted. ....

35. The rules are designed to **eliminate** obstacles that may discourage investors. ....

36.   Everyone believed that the results of his research would **surpass** their expectations.
       ....

37.   Not all foodstuffs that **come** from animals are properly tested to ensure they are fit for human
       consumption. ....

Down (⇩)

accuse	affect	assist	create	demand	elicit	endure	forbid
gather	handle	hasten	launch	mirror	misuse	oblige	obtain
permit	refuse						

1.   I don't know who broke your computer, but you can't **blame** me because I haven't been anywhere
       near it. ....

3.   He was asked to **deal with** the situation with tact and discretion. ....

7.   To **make** a new folder, click on the new folder icon at the top of your computer.
       ....

8.   We were unable to **obtain** the information we needed from the committee.
       ....

9.   There was general approval when the announcement to **ban** smoking on college premises was
       made. ....

10.   His inability to act quickly enough will probably **accelerate** their decision to dismiss him.
       ....

12.   Even a small change in economic circumstances can **influence** our spending habits.
       ....

14.   Alternative therapies are often suggested for patients who **reject** conventional medical treatment.
       ....

17.   The report was based on information that they managed to **collect** from all parts of the country.
       ....

18.   The college rules **require** students to refrain from smoking and drinking inside the faculty buildings.
       ....

20.   Trends come and go, but there are a few that will always **stay**. ....

22.   To ask for a loan, you will need to **acquire** a form from the student welfare office.
       ....

24.   It is often argued that not enough laws exist to punish those who **abuse** the Internet.
       ....

26.   The new technique will **facilitate** rapid identification of possible threats from unstable areas.
       ....

28.   The company announced it will **introduce** a new version of its software in January.
       ....

30.   The senator's relaxed attitude to the problem didn't **reflect** those of his constituents.
       ....

31.   The governor was asked to **insist on** new measures to combat crime. ....

34.   We do not **allow** the use of mobile phones in the building. ....

Similar meanings: Verbs 2

Rearrange the letters in **bold** at the end of sentences 1 – 16 to make words with the same or a similar meaning to the underlined words and expressions in the sentence. Write your answers in the spaces on the right. The shaded letter in each space is the same as the letter in the **bold** square in the next line. The first one has been done for you.

1. The machine was designed to grind rocks for industrial purposes. **srhcu**

    | c | r | u | s | h |

2. The television campaign helped to increase public awareness of the drug problem. **iehthnge**

    | h | | | | | |

3. During the election, the Republicans made a great effort to woo younger voters. **tactart**

4. Many retail outlets are substituting cashiers with automatic machines. **nelarcpig**

5. The new building symbolizes modern American architecture at its best. **pefeliixems**

6. Everyone endorsed the treaty as it was critically important to the peace process. **redpupost**

7. If you want to reclaim the money you have lost, you will have to fill in a claims form. **evroerc**

8. He was asked to account for the changes he had made to the curriculum. **pinelax**

9. More must be done to find other sources of fuel for when we deplete our supply of oil. **hatesxu**

10. It can take a lot of time and effort to acquire the grade you want in the TOEFL®. **hiveace**

11. Violence may have been averted if the police had not acted so aggressively. **vredntepe**

12. The media liked to depict the leader as a national hero, when in fact he was a cruel tyrant. **rpryato**

13. We know that there are benefits, but they are very difficult to quantify. **sumreea**

14. The aim of the organization is to promote travel among young people. **oragnceue**

15. The two reports emphasize the problems that are faced by those living in housing projects. **gighihlth**

16. The transformation is accelerated by adding salt to the solution. **satheden**

Exercise 2
Now do the same with these.

1. The study <u>confirmed</u> the findings of earlier research.
vopdre

p	r	o	v	e	d

2. No one was able to <u>unravel</u> the complex mystery surrounding her sudden disappearance. **vleos**

3. Travel can <u>broaden</u> your knowledge of the world around you. **senciare**

4. We wanted to <u>involve</u> the community in our plans for a new sports center. **ludecin**

5. Their choice was <u>influenced and controlled</u> by political circumstances. **tatdidce**

6. If you fail to attend classes, you might <u>lose</u> your right to continue studying at the college. **oeirftf**

7. The exhibition was originally <u>conceived</u> as a tribute to the Bauhaus movement. **tcedare**

8. The drug was designed to <u>regulate</u> the flow of blood to the brain. **tcoonlr**

9. The government is committed to <u>promoting</u> the use of public transport. **gagcuenrino**

10. Wind, tides, and the sun can all be used to <u>generate</u> power. **douprec**

11. We began to <u>think</u> that the project might involve more work than we had planned. **cpustse**

12. Thousands of young men volunteered to <u>defend</u> their country. **totprec**

13. Planning regulations <u>limited</u> development on the land outside large towns and cities. **acostrnidne**

14. They <u>tolerated</u> poor working conditions in order to finish the job quickly. **petacdec**

15. Before they began, they needed to <u>ascertain</u> that the project was feasible. **cehkc**

16. Some materials may <u>display</u> the characteristics of both a liquid and a solid. **itehxib**

Exercise 3
Finally, do the same with these.

1. We quickly <u>perceived</u> the truth about their intentions regarding the environment. **lredzaie**

| r | e | a | l | i | z | e | d |

2. Under his reign peace and mutual understanding <u>flourished</u>. **popederrs**

| | r | | | | | | |

3. The results <u>exceeded</u> everyone's expectations. **spsuareds**

4. Political apathy could be <u>interpreted</u> as a sign of satisfaction with the government. **dusneotodr**

5. The new drug considerably <u>enhanced</u> the patients' quality of life. **vimodpre**

6. Governments have been slow to <u>deal with</u> the problems of global warming. **srsaded**

7. They are trying to gather all the facts <u>pertaining</u> to the problem. **tirelagn**

8. The concept of factory outlet shopping <u>began</u> in the United States. **giniaoredt**

9. The foundation was formed specifically to <u>administer</u> the project. **gaamen**

10. Scientists <u>analyzed</u> samples of leaves taken from the area. **meaienxd**

11. Many people are reluctant to <u>eliminate</u> certain food products from their diet. **ervmeo**

12. We all <u>assumed</u> that he would leave when the project was finished. **pedospus**

13. The research failed to <u>yield</u> the information they were looking for. **ocpredu**

14. We didn't <u>accomplish</u> much this week. **vehiace**

15. The crisis was <u>resolved</u> through a series of open talks and compromise. **tlsedte**

16. The company pioneered the idea of selling cars that customers had to <u>assemble</u> themselves. **diubl**

Spelling

Exercise 1

Each passage below contains 12 words which have been spelt incorrectly. <u>Underline</u> the words, then write their correct spelling in the box below.

1.

Despite banning tobacco <u>advertiseing</u> and rising the price of cigarrettes, the goverment's anti-smoking campain has failed to have any long-term affects. It is now widely beleived that more drastic measures are neccessary. A new national comittee, which has been formed to tackle the proplem, has made several reccomendations. These include banning smoking in all public areas, and denying hospital treatment to persistant smokers who have been warned by their doctors to give up but failed to do so.

advertising			

2.

It is <u>argueable</u> wether good pronounciation is more important than good grammer and vocabulery. Consientious students balance their aquisition of these skills, hopeing to acheive both fluency and accuracey. English teachers should encourage there students to practice all the relevant language skills, and use their English at every oportunity.

arguable			

3.

It is <u>becomming</u> increasingly dificult for many people to find decent accomodation in the city at a price they can afford. To put it simpley, there are to many people and not enough homes for them. Local comunity centers and charitable organizeations such as Home Front can offer advise, but it is widely agreed that the situation is no longer managable. The fact that some councils in the city are building cheap, tempory housing for lower-paid profesionals is the only official acknowlegment of this problem.

becomming			

Exercise 2

Here are some more words which students of English (and many native English speakers) often spell incorrectly. Can you identify and correct the mistake in each case? Be careful: 3 of the words are spelt correctly!

1. reversable   2. proffessional   3. critisize   4. neccesary

5. begining   6. percieve   7. indespensable   8. refering

9. liason   10. tendancy   11. definately   12. embarass

13. address   14. recommend   15. responsable   16. seperate

17. questionaire   18. miniscule   19. intergrate   20. categories

21. wierd   22. iresistible   23. acheivement   24. millenium

25. occurence   26. independant   27. supercede   28. harrassment

Starting and stopping

Exercise 1

The box below contains 37 nouns, verbs, and phrasal verbs related to starting or stopping something. You will find these by reading from left to right (⇨) and from right to left (⇦), following the direction of the arrows. Identify as many as you can, and write them in the second box.

Start ⇨	A	B	O	L	I	S	H	A	R	I	S	E	B	A	C	K	⇨
⇦	S	O	L	C	E	S	A	E	C	L	E	C	N	A	C	T	U	O	⇦
⇩	U	R	E	D	E	L	E	T	E	D	E	T	E	R	D	I	S	C	⇨
⇦	S	S	I	D	S	S	I	M	S	I	D	E	U	N	I	T	N	O	⇦
⇩	U	A	D	E	E	M	B	A	R	K	E	R	A	D	I	C	A	T	⇨
⇦	R	I	F	L	E	P	X	E	H	S	I	L	B	A	T	S	E	E	⇦
⇩	E	F	R	E	E	Z	E	I	N	C	E	P	T	I	O	N	I	N	⇨
⇦	C	N	U	A	L	F	F	O	K	C	I	K	E	T	A	I	T	I	⇦
⇩	H	O	U	T	B	R	E	A	K	P	H	A	S	E	I	N	P	H	⇨
⇦	O	L	L	U	P	T	N	E	V	E	R	P	T	U	O	E	S	A	⇦
⇩	U	T	Q	U	A	S	H	Q	U	I	T	R	E	S	I	G	N	R	⇨
⇦	U	S	P	U	T	E	S	F	F	O	T	E	S	E	R	I	T	E	⇦
⇩	P	P	R	E	S	S	S	U	S	P	E	N	D	T	A	K	E	O	⇨
Finish	N	W	O	D	N	R	U	T	P	U	E	K	A	T	F	F	⇦

The words and phrases in the box above are:

Exercise 2

Now use the words and phrases to complete these sentences. In many cases, these sentences can be completed with more than one of the words / phrases. In the case of the verbs, you will need to change the form of some of them (for example, by adding -ed to the end). The first one has been done as an example.

1. Unfortunately, this afternoon's seminar on the Middle East has been .... *canceled* .... because the speaker is ill.

2. I can't find the document anywhere on my computer. I must have accidentally .... it.

3. The laboratory was forced to end its research project when the sponsoring company .... and refused to give it any more money.

4. Because of an .... of food poisoning recently, the school cafeteria will be closed until further notice.

5. The company was .... in 2009, but had to close down less than a year later.

6. Before .... on a long journey, it is very important to make sure you have everything you need.

7. Several of the airline's crews told the press that they were concerned about the safety of its aircraft, but the airline's owner managed to .... the story before it went public.

8. As a result of increased security and a bigger police presence, crime has been almost completely ....

9. The library installed security cameras to .... students from taking books without checking them out at the counter, but without much success.

10. We tried to .... the manager from making changes to the company structure, but he said he had already .... the first stage of the plan.

11. When the product was first .... onto the market in 1991, there was little public interest. However, after a concerted marketing campaign, sales rapidly ....

12. Owing to technical problems, use of the college IT center has been temporarily .... while the computers are checked for viruses.

13. I .... photography as a hobby when I was 13, but by the time I was 15 I had already decided to make it my career.

14. The new regulations will not all begin at once: they will be gradually .... over the next two years. Meanwhile, the old system will be gradually ....

15. Between its .... in 1925 and its eventual .... in 2002, World Film Studios made over 300 movies.

16. Hostilities between the major powers .... in November 1977 after a peace treaty was signed.

17. Professor Vettriano is 64, so I guess he'll be .... soon. I think he'll miss working here, though.

18. I had had enough of working there and was about to tell my boss I was going to .... when she called me into her office and told me I was ....!

19. They made an excellent offer, but we were obliged to .... it .... because we were working on too many other projects. (*Complete this sentence with one phrasal verb*)

20. Course fees have risen rapidly over the last three years, but last week the college announced a ....; they have promised no more fee increases until the end of next year.

21. The student book discount program has been .... From now on, students will have to pay the full price for all their books.

22. When Congress agreed to .... the old tax laws, smaller companies suddenly found themselves much better off.

23. We have a lot of things to discuss at this meeting, so I suggest we .... immediately with a report on last year's sales.

24. Several problems have .... recently as a result of staff illness. One of these is that fact that two courses we had planned are no longer going to go ahead.

25. Five students have been .... from the college for vandalism.

Task commands

Exercise 1

Look at the list of tasks in sentences 1 – 8. In particular, look at the words and phrases in **bold**, which are telling the writer / speaker what he / she must do. Match these words with a suitable definition of the task command in A – H. The first one has been done for you.

1.   **Account for** the increased use of social networking on the Internet. ......*F*...

2.   **Analyze** the effects of climate change around the world. ....

3.   **Evaluate** the improvements you have made to your English since you started using this book. ....

4.   **Compare** and **contrast** the two machines. ....

5.   **Define** 'happiness', and say how important it is. ....

6.   **Demonstrate** the different features on this cellphone. ....

7.   **Discuss** the advantages and disadvantages of growing up in a big city. ....

8.   **Elaborate on** your feelings about global capitalism. ....

A.   Give the meaning of something.
B.   Talk about something with someone else, or write about it from different viewpoints.
C.   Calculate the value, importance, or effect of something.
D.   Explain something closely and scientifically.
E.   Explain something in more detail than you did previously.
F.   Say why something has happened or is happening.
G.   Show how something works, usually by physically operating it so that the other person knows what it does and how it works.
H.   Look at two things side by side to see in what way they are similar and / or different.

Exercise 2

Now do the same with these.

1.   **Estimate** the costs of setting up a Web site for the school. ....

2.   **Examine** the causes of global warming. ....

3.   **Illustrate** the problems caused by the increased use of private vehicles. ....

4.   **Justify** your reasons for only considering one aspect of the problem. ....

5.   **Outline** your country's environmental policy. ....

6.   **Predict** the changes that we are going to see in information technology in the next ten years. ....

7.   **Suggest** ways in which food shortages in some countries could be solved. ....

8.   **Trace** the development of space travel since the 1960s. ....

A.   Explain, with real examples, why something has happened or is happening.
B.   Say what you think is going to happen in the future.
C.   Describe what you think can be done in order to achieve something.
D.   Calculate (but not exactly) the value or cost of something.
E.   Give the main points of something, or a broad description of something, without giving too much detail.
F.   Give a brief history of something, in the order in which it happened.
G.   Write or talk about the different aspects (e.g., causes, results) of something.
H.   Show that you have a good reason for doing something, especially if other people think you have done something wrong or bad.

Time

Exercise 1
Use the words and phrases in the boxes to complete the sentences. Pay particular attention to the words that come before and/or after the gap in each sentence.

Part 1: One action or situation occurring before another action or situation

by the time   earlier   formerly   precede   previously   prior to

1. .... the advent of the Industrial Revolution, pollution was virtually unheard of.

2. .... the army had restored order, the city had been almost completely devastated.

3. .... known as Bombay, Mumbai is India's most vibrant and exciting city.

4. A sudden drop in temperature will usually .... a blizzard.

5. It was my first trip on an airplane. .... I'd always gone by train.

6. The President made a speech praising charity organizations working in Mozambique. .... that day he had promised massive economic aid to stricken areas.

Part 2: One action or situation occurring at the same time as another action

at that very moment   during   in the meantime   while

1. .... the Senator was making his speech, thousands of demonstrators took to the streets.

2. .... the speech they jeered and shouted slogans.

3. The Senator continued speaking. .... the police were ordered onto the streets.

4. He praised the police for their restrained behavior. ...., they began attacking the demonstrators with batons and tear gas.

Part 3: One action or situation occurring after another action or situation

afterwards   as soon as   following

1. .... the earthquake, emergency organizations around the world swung into action.

2. .... the stock market collapsed, there was panic buying on an unprecedented scale.

3. The Klondike gold rush lasted from 1896 to 1910. .... the area became practically deserted overnight.

Exercise 2

Look at the words and phrases in the box below and decide if we usually use them to talk about (1) the past, (2) the past leading to the present, (3) the present or (4) the future.

> a few decades ago   as things stand   at the turn of the century
> at that point / moment in history   back in the 1990s   between 2003 and 2005
> by the end of this year   ever since   for the foreseeable future   for the next few weeks
> for the past few months   from 2006 to 2011   from now on   in another five years' time
> in medieval times   in my childhood / youth   in those days   last century   lately
> nowadays   one day   over the coming weeks and months   over the past six weeks
> sooner or later   these days

Exercise 3

There are a lot of idioms and other phrases that use the word '*time*' in English. In this exercise, you should match the first part of each sentence on the left with its second part on the right, using the phrases in **bold** to help you.

1. I'm very busy at the moment, but I'll try to **make**…	(a) … **time warp**.
2. Don is a really nice man. I **have a lot of**…	(b) … **times out of ten** she's punctual.
3. Susanna is so old-fashioned. She seems to be **living in a**…	(c) … **time for everything**, I suppose.
4. I would love a holiday, but I never seem to **find**…	(d) … **the time comes**.
5. We thought we would be late, but we arrived **with**…	(e) … **time**, too.
6. Shall we start now? After all, **there's no**…	(f) … **the time**.
7. At last, here comes our bus. **About**…	(g) … **time being**.
8. Chris is sometimes late, but **nine**…	(h) … **time to time** it can be glorious.
9. We really need to hurry. There's **no**…	(i) … **time will tell**.
10. I don't want to make a decision now; I'll decide **when**…	(j) … **the times**.
11. I don't know if we will be successful; **only**…	(k) … **time now**.
12. I'm not really watching this movie; I'm just **killing**…	(l) … **time around**.
13. If the company is going to compete successfully, we will need to **move with**…	(m) … **his time**.
14. I've never had Japanese food before, but **there's a first**…	(n) … **time to spare**.
15. If we don't win this time, we will the **second**…	(o) … **time for** him.
16. Picasso was a remarkable artist who was years **ahead of**…	(p) … **time** until my friends arrive.
17. Winters here are generally cold and gray, but **from**…	(q) … **the time** to see you later.
18. I'm thinking of changing jobs in the future, but I'll continue working here **for the**…	(r) … **time to lose**.
19. This isn't a sudden decision. I've been thinking of moving **for some**…	(s) … **the time** for one.
20. My students just aren't interested in their lessons. They don't even listen to me **half**…	(t) … **time like the present**.

Word association: Adjectives

Complete the sentences with an adjective from the box. This adjective should be one that is often used (i.e., it *collocates*) with the nouns and / or adverbs in *italics* in the sentence. To help you, there is a sample sentence to show you how that adjective could work with one of the nouns or adverbs. The first one has been done as an example.

careful	central	critical	damaging	essential	false	~~important~~
impossible	interested	lengthy	major	material	modest	noticeable
objective	particular	popular	positive	rapid	rational	realistic	severe

1. ....*Important*............. is often followed by the nouns *aspect, element, factor, feature, issue, part,* or *point*. It is often preceded by the adverbs *crucially, extremely, particularly, terribly,* or *vitally*.

   (Sample sentence: *It is vitally important to disconnect the appliance from the power supply before dismantling it*).

2. .... is often followed by the nouns *goods, possessions, prosperity, resources, rewards, wealth,* or *well-being*.

   (Sample sentence: *He believed in the principles of life, liberty, and the pursuit of _____ wealth*).

3. .... is often followed by the nouns *analysis, assessment, description, evaluation,* or *measurement*. It is often preceded by the adverbs *completely, entirely, purely, totally, truly,* or *wholly*.

   (Sample sentence: *We tried to keep a purely _____ record of what we heard and saw*).

4. .... is often followed by the nouns *breakthrough, pause, change, concern, contribution, drawback, factor, influence, obstacle, problem, setback, source,* or *upheaval*.

   (Sample sentence: *The withdrawal of sponsorship was a _____ setback to our plans*).

5. .... is often followed by the nouns *argument, aspect, debate, feature, idea, importance, issue, role,* or *theme*.

   (Sample sentence: *The _____ theme of his talk was the possibility of interstellar travel*).

6. .... is often followed by the nouns *approach, argument, choice, decision, explanation, hypothesis,* or *thought*.

   (Sample sentence: *We need to make a _____ choice that is based on our needs and on our available funds*).

7. .... is often followed by the nouns *consequence, effect, impact, result, admission, allegation, criticism,* or *disclosure*.

   (Sample sentence: *After a series of _____ allegations about his professional misconduct, he resigned*).

8. .... is often followed by the nouns *change, decline, deterioration, expansion, growth, increase, progress, rise,* or *succession*.

   (Sample sentence: *The computer industry went through several _____ changes when the Internet was introduced to the public for the first time*).

9. .... is often followed by the nouns *accusation, allegation, assumption, belief, claim, description, impression,* or *statement*. It is often preceded by the adverbs *blatantly, completely, entirely, patently, totally,* or *utterly*.

   (Sample sentence: *She made several _____ assumptions about her new professor*).

10. .... is often followed by the nouns *analysis, assessment, consideration, deliberation, examination, observation,* or *planning*.

(Sample sentence: *After _____ observation, we noticed that the drug was beginning to take effect*).

11. .... is often followed by the nouns *belief, misconception, myth, opinion,* or *view*.

(Sample sentence: *It is a _____ misconception that men are better drivers than women*).

12. .... is often followed by the nouns *analysis, appraisal, evaluation, examination,* or *scrutiny*.

(Sample sentence: *They carried out a _____ examination of the documents to see if they were genuine*).

13. .... is often followed by the nouns *attention, concern, emphasis, importance, need, relevance,* or *significance*.

(Sample sentence: *When you are writing an essay, you should pay _____ attention to cohesion of ideas*).

14. .... is often followed by the nouns *characteristic, component, element, feature, ingredient, part,* or *requirement*.

(Sample sentence: *A working knowledge of Spanish is an _____ requirement if you want the job*).

15. .... is often preceded by the adverbs *comparatively, fairly, quite, rather, relatively, suitably, surprisingly,* or *very*.

(Sample sentence: *Everyone said he was arrogant and boastful, but when I interviewed him, I found him to be surprisingly _____ about his achievements*).

16. .... is often preceded by the adverbs *absolutely, almost, nearly, practically, quite, seemingly, totally, utterly,* or *virtually*.

(Sample sentence: *I found the language practically _____ to learn*).

17. .... is often preceded by the adverbs *deeply, extremely, genuinely, mainly, particularly, primarily, principally,* or *seriously*.

(Sample sentence: *I like nineteenth-century art, but I'm primarily _____ in the pre-Raphaelite movement*).

18. .... is often followed by the nouns *approach, attitude, feedback, outlook, reinforcement, response,* or *view*.

(Sample sentence: *His presentation was well-received, and he got a lot of _____ feedback*).

19. .... is often followed by the nouns *change, difference, drop, improvement,* or *increase*.

(Sample sentence: *There has been a _____ increase in the cost of living over the last three years*).

20. .... is often followed by the nouns *delay, discussion, interview, negotiations, pause,* or *period*.

(Sample sentence: *After a _____ pause, she continued speaking*).

21. .... is often followed by the nouns *difficulty, hardship, problem, recession, setback, shortage,* or *threat*.

(Sample sentence: *Earlier settlers in the region faced _____ hardship, and many died young from illness and starvation*).

22. .... is often followed by the nouns *alternative, assessment, attitude, chance, estimate, expectation, goal, option, prospect, target,* or *view*.

(Sample sentence: *When you are studying for the TOEFL®, you should try to set yourself _____ targets, and not try to do too much too quickly*).

Word association: Nouns

Rearrange the letters in **bold** to make nouns. These nouns should collocate with the verbs, adjectives, and other words in *italics* in the sentences. To help you, the first letter of each noun is <u>underlined</u>. Write your answers in the crossword on page 70. The first one has been done as an example.

<u>Across</u> (⇨)

1. **a<u>B</u>krgcdonu** is often preceded by the words *cultural, disadvantaged, educational, ethnic, middle-class, privileged, religious, social,* or *working class*.

5. An action can have a / an *adverse, beneficial, cumulative, damaging, detrimental, dramatic, harmful, immediate, major, negative, positive, profound, serious, significant,* or *substantial* **cf<u>e</u>fte** on something.

7. When they speak, a person might have a *broad, heavy, pronounced, strong, thick,* or *unmistakable* **ce<u>a</u>ctn**.

8. If you are not sure about the answer to a question, you can take a / an *educated, good, informed, inspired, lucky, rough,* or *wild* **esgsu**.

11. You can *accept, ask for, follow, get, give, ignore, obtain, offer, provide, receive, take,* or *want* **v<u>a</u>cedi** to or from someone.

12. You can give a problem *careful, detailed, due,* or *serious* **tiera<u>c</u>oidonns**.

14. A **esggsuonti** can be *constructive, helpful, positive, practical, sensible,* or *tentative*. You can *adopt, make, offer, oppose, reject, submit, volunteer,* or *welcome* one of these.

15. You can *disobey, disregard, follow, give, ignore, issue, obey, provide,* or *repeat* an **ti<u>i</u>nstonruc**.

17. A **uton<u>s</u>oli** to a problem or dispute can be *ideal, optimal, peaceful, possible, practical, satisfactory, simple,* or *workable*.

19. You can *ask, deny, gain, get, give, grant, obtain, receive, refuse, request,* or *seek* **sieomiprsn** to do something.

20. You can *encounter, experience, face, find,* or *have* **d<u>i</u>ulfctyfi** with something.

21. A **uaonficaqtili** can be *academic, educational, formal, professional, specialist,* or *vocational*. You can *acquire, gain, get, have, hold, obtain,* or *possess* one of these.

22. **<u>O</u>pryuptiotn** is often preceded by the adjectives *ample, excellent, golden, great, ideal, lost, missed, perfect, rare,* or *unique*. It is also often preceded by the verbs *miss, offer, provide, seize,* or *take*.

25. When you are trying to guess or calculate something, you can make a / an *accurate, conservative, realistic, reliable,* or *rough* **st<u>e</u>imeat**.

29. A product or a person can have *broad, mass, popular, universal,* or *wide* **p<u>a</u>alpe**.

32. You can *collect, destroy, gather,* or *produce* **ide<u>e</u>venc** that something has been done. This can be *admissible, circumstantial, conclusive, incriminating, sufficient,* or *supporting*.

33. **<u>M</u>enecidi** can be *alternative, complementary, conventional, herbal, holistic, orthodox,* or *traditional*.

34. When you do something, you usually have a / an *compelling, good, legitimate, logical, main, major, obvious, simple,* or *valid* **er<u>n</u>sao** for doing it.

Down (⇩)

2. If you are not careful, or if you are unlucky, you might be involved in a *bad, fatal, horrific, minor, nasty, serious,* or *tragic* **de_a_cntci**.

3. You can *accept, assume, bear, exercise, fulfill, shoulder,* or *take* **po_r_etysnsilibi** for your (or someone else's) actions.

4. You can *conclude, negotiate, reach, secure,* or *sign* an **g_a_rcnctmc**.

6. An object can have *distinctive, important, interesting, key, main, special, striking,* or *unusual* **tuf_e_esar**.

9. If someone has a rather 'negative' personality, their **av_b_eiohr** can be *aggressive, antisocial, bad, disruptive, insulting, threatening,* or *violent*.

10. You can have a *brilliant, checkered, distinguished, glittering, promising, successful,* or *varied* **re_c_ear**.

12. When you work as part of a team, you can make a *great, huge, important, major, outstanding, positive, significant, useful,* or *valuable* **utib_c_oninotr** to the team and its activities.

13. You can give a / an *accurate, brief, detailed, full, general, vague,* or *vivid* **ponde_r_itisc** of something.

16. **sciC_r_miti** of something (for example, a book or the actions of a politician) can be *adverse, fierce, outspoken, severe, strong,* or *widespread*.

18. You can *conduct, demand, launch, order, require,* or *undertake* an **tiga_i_esnvtino** into something.

23. For actions and achievements, you can *command, deserve, earn, gain, have, lose, show,* or *win* **pct_e_res**. This can be *considerable, deep, genuine, healthy, mutual,* or *proper*.

24. When doing something complicated, you can *adopt, apply, choose, develop, devise, employ, pioneer, provide,* or *use* a **ehtm_d_o** that makes it easier or more effective.

26. A **qeenc_s_ue** can be *alphabetical, chronological, logical, numerical,* or *random*.

27. A **gmjutend** can be *affected, delivered, exercised, formed, given, impaired, made, passed, reserved,* or *suspended*.

28. You can undertake a / an *ambitious, collaborative, individual, innovative, joint, major, minor,* or *special* **ct_p_reoj**.

30. You can *assess, chart, check, evaluate, follow, hamper, hinder, impede, monitor, obstruct, review, slow, track,* or *watch* the **prsorseg** of something.

31. If someone does something wrong, you might teach them a *hard, harsh, important, salutary,* or *valuable* **sol_e_ns**.

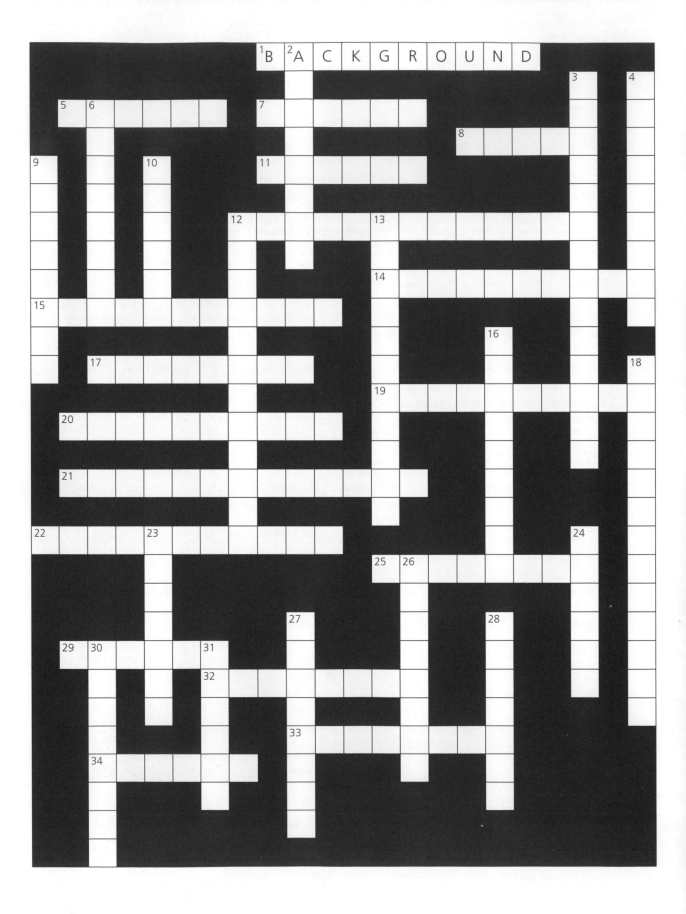

Word association: Verbs

Exercise 1
Complete each of the following sentences with one verb. This verb should be one that is often used (i.e., it *collocates*) with the nouns and / or adverbs in *italics*. To help you, the first and last letters of each word have been given to you, and there is a sample sentence to show you how that verb could work with one of the nouns or adverbs.

Write your answers in the appropriate spaces in the grid. If you do this correctly, you will reveal a word in the shaded vertical strip that is often used with one of these nouns: *authority, confidence, credibility, legitimacy, morale, positions,* or *stability* (for example, 'He's very worried about his exams, so we don't want to do anything that might _____ his confidence any further').

1.   You can i...e someone's or something's *behavior, choice, decision, development, outcome,* or *policy*.
(Sample sentence: *I don't want to _____ your decision in any way*).

2.   You can o...n *approval, authorization, consent, evidence, funding, information, license,* or *permission*.
(Sample sentence: *You need to _____ permission to use the computers in the library*).

3.   You can d...s an *issue, a matter, a plan, a proposal, a question, a subject,* or *a topic*.
(Sample sentence: *We're all very tired. I suggest we _____ the matter tomorrow*).

4.   You can s...e *an argument, a conflict, a dispute, a quarrel,* or *your differences*.
(Sample sentence: *Neither side showed any willingness to _____ the dispute*).

5.   You can *actively, greatly, positively,* or *strongly* e...e someone or something.
(Sample sentence: *When I was young, my parents actively _____ me to read as much as possible*).

6.   You can c...y with a *demand, legislation, an order, a regulation, a request, a requirement,* or *a rule*.
(Sample sentence: *You are legally obliged to _____ with the regulations*).

7.   You can d...e *a mechanism, a method, a plan, a scheme, a strategy,* or *a system*.
(Sample sentence: *He _____ a cunning plan to help his friend*).

8.   You can u...r *a conspiracy, evidence, a fact, a fraud, a mystery, a plot, a scandal, a secret,* or *the truth*.
(Sample sentence: *The investigation _____ a scandal that would bring down the government*).

9.   You can d...e *credit, a mention, praise, recognition, respect,* or *support*.
(Sample sentence: *They _____ a lot of praise for all their hard work*).

Exercise 2

Follow the same instructions as Exercise 1. This time, the word you will reveal in the shaded vertical strip is one that is often used with the nouns *agreement, ceasefire, contract, deal, price, settlement, terms, treaty,* or *truce* (for example, '*After the unions refused to end the strike, the management attempted to _____ a new contract*').

1. You can i...e *affection, awe, confidence, devotion, envy, loyalty,* or *respect* in other people.
   (Sample sentence: *His actions did little to _____ confidence in his friends and colleagues*).

2. You can o...t *bitterly, formally, strenuously, strongly, vehemently,* or *vigorously* about something.
   (Sample sentence: *She _____ vehemently when she was accused of cheating*).

3. You can a...e *consistently, convincingly, forcefully, passionately, persuasively, plausibly,* or *strongly* for or about something.
   (Sample sentence: *They _____ forcefully for a change to the existing rules*).

4. You can o...e something *bitterly, fiercely, implacably, strenuously, strongly, vehemently,* or *vigorously.*
   (Sample sentence: *Darwin's theories are still bitterly _____ by many people*).

5. You can f...t *corruption, crime, discrimination, prejudice,* or *terrorism.* You can do this *desperately, doggedly, hard, stubbornly,* or *tenaciously.*
   (Sample sentence: *The new government promised the electorate that it would _____ corruption at all levels*).

6. You can h...t *a danger, a difference, a difficulty, a fact, the importance (of something), an issue, a need (for something), the plight (of something), a problem,* or *a weakness.*
   (Sample sentence: *Her report _____ the plight of migrant workers in the state*).

7. You can c...e something or someone *completely, considerably, dramatically, drastically, fundamentally, radically,* or *significantly.*
   (Sample sentence: *Global warming is believed to have radically _____ the climate in some parts of the world*).

8. You can u...e *an analysis, an assessment, an investigation, a program, a project, research, a review, a study, a survey,* or *a task.*
   (Sample sentence: *The board promised to _____ a review of current working practices*).

9. Something or someone can d...r *considerably, greatly, markedly, radically, sharply, significantly, substantially,* or *widely* from something or someone else.
   (Sample sentence: *English _____ markedly from Spanish in that the words are not always pronounced as they are written*).

Exercise 3

Follow the same instructions as Exercises 1 and 2. This time, the word you will reveal in the shaded vertical strip is one that is often used with the nouns *attitude*, *belief*, *idea*, *impression*, *notion*, *stereotype*, *tendency*, *trend*, or *view* (for example, 'The latest figures _____ the view that young people read less than they used to').

1. You can *heartily, thoroughly, warmly, wholeheartedly, officially, overwhelmingly, personally,* or *unanimously* a...e of someone or something.
    (Sample sentence. *We wholeheartedly _____ the measures that you have taken to boost morale*).

2. You can l...n to something or someone *attentively, carefully, closely, hard, intently,* or *closely.*
    (Sample sentence: *_____ carefully, because I will say this only once*).

3. You can d...s an allegation, a claim, an idea, a notion, a suggestion, or *a theory.*
    (Sample sentence: *She _____ my allegation as a complete fabrication, and more or less accused me of lying*).

4. You can a...n *a belief, a claim, a commitment, a concept, an idea, a policy,* or *a principle.*
    (Sample sentence: *He used to be quite religious, but _____ his beliefs when his wife died in a road accident*).

5. Something can f...l *dramatically, rapidly, sharply, slightly, steadily,* or *steeply.*
    (Sample sentence: *Unemployment figures _____ dramatically under the government's Work or Starve initiative*).

6. You can c...t *crime, discrimination, disease, fraud, inflation, poverty, racism, terrorism, unemployment,* or *violence.*
    (Sample sentence: *The organization's main mission statement is to _____ disease and poverty In developing nations*).

7. Someone or something can u...e *a difficulty, a fact, the importance (of something), the need (for something), a point, a problem,* or *the significance (of something).*
    (Sample sentence: *The survey results _____ the need for change in people's attitudes toward the homeless*).

8. You can c...e *an agreement, a contract, a deal, a pact,* or *a treaty.*
    (Sample sentence: *At the end of the summit, an agreement was _____ under which trade sanctions between both countries would be lifted*).

9. You can o...e *a barrier, a difficulty, a disadvantage, a fear, a hurdle, limitations, an obstacle, a problem, resistance,* or *a weakness.*
    (Sample sentence: *Hypnosis helped him to _____ his fear of flying*).

1.										
2.										
3.										
4.										
5.										
6.										
7.										
8.										
9.										

Word forms: Nouns from verbs

The verbs in the top box can all be made into nouns by removing and / or adding letters. Decide on the noun form of each verb, and then write it (in its noun form) in the appropriate section of the table, depending on the changes that are made to it. There are <u>five words</u> for <u>each section</u> of the table, and there are <u>10 words</u> that <u>do not fit</u> into any section of the table.

abolish	acquire	admire*	apply*	argue	arrive	assure	attend
behave	choose	coincide	compete	consult*	consume*	criticize*	
decide	determine	disturb	emphasize	expand	expect	expose	fail
identify	imply	intervene	labor	lose	maintain	manage*	
negotiate*	notify	permit	persuade	prefer	produce*	prohibit	
promote*	provide	qualify*	recognize	recommend	refuse	rehearse	
relax	require	respond	scrutinize	sign	solve	subscribe*	suggest
supervise*	survive*	warn					

* Note: <u>NOT</u> the person who does these things (i.e., *admirer, applicant, consultant, consumer, critic, laborer, manager, negotiator, producer, promoter, provider, qualifier, subscriber, supervisor, survivor*)

Remove 2 letters, then add 4 letters:	(Example: conclude → conclu~~de~~ → conclu<u>sion</u>)
Remove 1 letter, then add 7 letters:	(Example: verify → veri~~fy~~ → verif<u>ication</u>)
Remove 1 letter, then add 5 letters:	(Example: examine → examin~~e~~ → examin<u>ation</u>)
Remove 1 letter, then add 4 letters:	(Example: reduce → reduc~~e~~ → reduc<u>tion</u>)
Remove 1 letter, then add 3 letters:	(Example: concentrate → concentrat~~e~~ → concentrat<u>ion</u>)
Remove 1 letter, then add 2 letters:	(Example: disperse → dispers~~e~~ → dispers<u>al</u>)

Add 3 letters:	(Example: depart → depart<u>ure</u>)
Add 4 letters:	Example: improve → improve<u>ment</u>)
Add 5 letters:	(Example: confirm → confirm<u>ation</u>)

Exercise 2

Now take the verbs from the box that did *not* fit into any of the sections in Exercise 1, change them into nouns and use them to complete these sentences. The words you need for the sentences appear in the same order as they do in the box.

1. I love collecting old things, and my latest .... is this 19th century perfume bottle.

2. Our college cafeteria offers an excellent .... of healthy, low-fat dishes.

3. I don't mind ...., as long as it's constructive and given in a nice way.

4. Restaurants should place greater .... on the quality of the food they serve rather than the quantity.

5. Many factories rely on a plentiful supply of cheap, reliable ....

6. The tragic .... of the Titanic in 1912 was a major blow to the shipbuilding industry in Belfast.

7. Modern commercial airliners require frequent ...., which can be very expensive.

8. Once you start making mistakes, you will find that your work comes under much closer .... to ensure you are maintaining standards.

9. I believe that solar energy offers a good, low-cost .... to our fuel problems.

10. The student social club requires its members to pay an annual .... of $50.

Word forms: Nouns from adjectives

Change the adjective in **bold** in each of these sentences to a noun so that the word is grammatically correct in the sentence. The first one has been done for you.

1. Items of **valuable** can be left in the safe at reception. ...._value_............

2. Money cannot make up for bad **tasteful** and bad manners. ....

3. Do you have a **thirsty** for knowledge? Then why not enroll on one of our evening college courses? ....

4. It is often said that '**honest** is the best policy'. ....

5   It can often be lack of **confident** that prevents a student from maximizing his or her potential. ....

6. Many people heading off to college for the first time are often unaware of the **expensive** involved in simple day-to-day life. ....

7. Student discounts are offered on most products and services on our Web site, although some **restricted** apply. ....

8. There were a few **similar** between the Boeing 727 and the Tupolev 154 airliners, but these were mainly cosmetic. ....

9. The Director of Studies is unable to say with any **certain** when the new changes will be implemented. ....

10. Unnecessary **absent** from work is costing American companies millions of dollars a year. ....

11. Please complete the form and return it at your earliest **convenient**. ....

12. The student union has questioned the **necessary** of CCTV in the library, but the management insists it is necessary in order to reduce petty theft. ....

13. Despite a **relaxed** of regulations, many feel that they are under too much pressure to conform to a set of outdated rules. ....

14. Sometimes in business, rules have to be changed according to needs: **flexible** is the key to success. ....

15. Health and **safe** issues should be a priority with any organization. ....

16. The management accepts no **responsible** for items lost or stolen in the cafeteria and immediate area. ....

17. In advertising, **accurate** is very important when it comes to identifying the target market. ....

18. The legal **professional** is often criticized for concentrating on making money instead of upholding the law. ....

19. There were several unforeseen **complicated** with the new airport extension owing to opposition from environmental groups. ....

20. Do you know the **different** between *net* profit and *gross* profit? Is *overtime* the same as *allowed time*? If you answered 'no' to the first and 'yes' to the second, it's time you joined our Business for Basics course! ....

21. His success and popularity were probably due in part to his wonderful **charismatic**.
....

22. There is a growing problem of drug **addicted** in our cities. ....

23. The US **constitutional** guarantees freedom of the press. ....

24. As soon as the **investigative** is complete, we can make a decision. ....

25. There can be no **justified** for paying health workers so little money. ....

26. By the time he was 30, he was no longer able to differentiate between fantasy and **real**.
....

Exercise 2

Change the adjectives in the box into nouns following the instructions in the table. Each instruction relates to <u>three</u> of the adjectives in the box. One has been done as an example.

able   aggressive   appreciative   available   aware   bored   ~~comfortable~~ compatible   confused   considerate   convenient   creative   deep familiar   fashionable   functional   high   hot   logical   long   loyal mature   optimistic   optional   pessimistic   popular   punctual   realistic secure   serious   strong   sufficient   systematic   true   warm   weak

Remove 4 letters:	comfort
Remove 3 letters, then add 5 letters:	
Remove 3 letters, then add 1 letter:	
Remove 2 letters, then add 5 letters:	
Remove 2 letters, then add 3 letters:	
Remove 2 letters, then add 2 letters:	
Remove 2 letters:	
Remove 1 letter, then add 3 letters:	
Remove 1 letter, then add 2 letters:	
Add 2 letters:	
Add 3 letters:	
Add 4 letters:	

Try to use some of the words above in some of your own sentences.

Word forms: Adjectives from verbs

Change the verbs in **bold** into their correct adjective form so that they are grammatically correct in the context of the sentences. The first two have been done for you.

1. At the recruitment drive we were shown a lot of **promote** material, but it wasn't very **inspire**.

   ....*promotional*.........   ....*inspiring*.........

2. Recently, there have been some **innovate** and **impress** plans to change the student social areas.

   ....

3. In the interests of the environment, we all need to change our **waste** habits, so the college is introducing an **oblige** code for recycling and cutting down on waste.

   ....

4. The task we were given was very **repeat** and as a result it quickly became very **bore**.

   ....

5. Everybody was very **excite** when we were told about the cultural trip to Paris, but I was a little **doubt** it would go ahead. ....

6. Our new Director of Studies isn't very **decide** and needs to play a more **act** role in the day-to-day running of the college. ....

7. Computer software designers need to be far more **invent** if they want to keep up with a changing and **change** market. ....

8. The Coke and coffee machines have both been out of order five times this week, and the air-conditioning hasn't been working for a month: these **continue** breakdowns, coupled with the **continue** heat, have resulted in a lot of short tempers.

   ....

9. My tutor isn't very **approach**: in fact, some of my fellow students find him a little bit **frighten**!

   ....

10. Her presentation wasn't very **convince**, and several of her classmates were extremely **criticize** of her arguments. ....

11. The market for all-**include** holidays (in which customers pay for their flight, accommodation, meals, and drinks in advance) has become very **compete**.

    ....

12. Our tutor is very **help** and **support**, but unfortunately he isn't very **depend**.

    ....

13. The mistake was easily **rectify**, but it would have been far more **prefer** if it hadn't happened in the first place. ....

14. Fees are non-**negotiate**, and you will need to pay a non-**refund** deposit of $500 before we can enroll you. ....

15. There is **restrict** access to the building, and all visitors will need to show a **validate** pass and some form of ID. ....

16. Participation in the evening training seminars is entirely **volunteer**, but we hope that everyone will attend these highly **construct** sessions.

    ....

17. The accident was **avoid**, and it wouldn't have happened if you hadn't been so **care**.

    ....

18. He's a very **create** and **imagine** artist, and his commitment to helping young painters is **admire**.

    ....

19. When you apply for a job, it is very important to be **specify** about your **occupy** qualifications, and any previous experience. ....

20. A good job should offer an **attract** salary and other **excel** benefits, such as a company car and free healthcare package. ....

Working words

Exercise 1

This exercise lets you review some of the more common 'grammar'-type words (prepositions, conjunctions, pronouns, prepositions, etc.). <u>Underline</u> the correct word or phrase in each **bold** pair in these sentences. Read the *whole* sentence first. In some cases, both words and / or phrases are correct.

1. I'm afraid **of / to** say you have absolutely **no / not** chance **for / of** passing the exam.

2. A few years **ago / before**, people **use / used** to write letters to each other. **Now / These** days, It's all e-mails and text messages.

3. You **can / may** leave early today **if / providing** you promise to work late tomorrow.

4. **Between / From** 2006 and 2008, the book sold **more / over** a million copies.

5. One or two of my friends live abroad, but **most / the most** of them live **close / near** my home.

6. Please **be / being** quiet. I'm trying to concentrate **at / on** my project.

7. **If / Unless** it rains tomorrow, we can go **for / on** a picnic.

8. We wanted to see the exhibition **at / on** the art gallery, but **knowing / realizing** how many other people **are / would** be there, we decided to give it a miss.

9. In **despite / spite** of missing most of his lessons, he **managed / succeeded** to pass the exam.

10. Teachers are **as / also** capable of making mistakes as **anybody / anyone** else.

11. I enjoy **to work / working** with people who come from a wide range of backgrounds. This is why I'm so keen **for / on** working for the UN.

12. Jan Kelly, a teacher **which / who** works at Park Green College in Boston, has **just / recently** been given a 'Teacher of the Year' award.

13. He approached his English lessons **in / with** enthusiasm, and **did / made** excellent progress as a result.

14. His sudden decision to leave the team took everyone **by / for** surprise, since previously he **had / was** been very interested in the project.

15. He spent the second half of his life living in **a / the** remote village of Hogstail Rise, **where / which** he wrote most of his novels.

16. **By / When** the time she retired, she **had / has** worked for the company for 32 years, and during **this / that** time, she only took one or two days **absent / off** sick.

17. We **lost / missed** the bus into town, so we had to walk instead, and by the time we got to the theater, we were **so / too** late to catch the beginning of the movie.

18. **How's / What's** my brother like? Well, he's **little / quite** friendly, and has a great sense of humor, but he is **also / as well** lazy and selfish.

<u>Exercise 2</u>

Now do the same with these.

1. Some people try to give **in / up** cigarettes by smoking **to / until** they feel sick, or by limiting themselves to one or **few / two** a day, but **these / those** methods are not very effective.

2. My English school, **which / who** is near the center of the city, is **a one / one** of the **best / better** language schools **at / in** the country.

3. There were at **least / less** 60 people in the room, which was far **extra / more** than the organizers expected, and **as / since** there were only 20 chairs, most of us **had / must** to stand.

4. In most respects he was a normal child, but **how / what** made him different **as / from** everybody **else / others** was his enthusiasm for solving complex mathematical puzzles.

5. On one hand I love **attending / going** to concerts, but on **another / the other** hand I get nervous in large crowds of people.

6. I've **been / being** working on this essay **during / for** over a week, but **any / no** matter how hard I try, I just can't seem to finish it.

7. Up **to / until** a few years ago, people **might / would** have the same career for life. Nowadays, **they / these** can reasonably expect to change careers two **and / or** three times.

8. In spite of **be / being** rather lazy, he is always able **can / to** get good results and has made **a / the** good impression **on / to** his tutors.

9. **Between / From** 2001 to 2004, unemployment figures dropped to an all-time low, **but / however** they then started climbing again, reaching **a / their** peak in 2009.

10. Students are **not / only** allowed to miss a class **in / on** condition that they inform **their / there** tutor at least three days in advance (**if / unless** they are ill, in which case they should try to call the college on the day **itself / themselves**).

11. Please come **at / on** time to your lessons, and **be / do** prepared to work **a lot / much** harder from now on.

12. He admitted **borrowing / to borrow** my camera without asking **about / for** my permission, but he vigorously denied **breaking / to break** it.

13. If you cause **a / any** damage to college property, whether **by / on** accident or **by / on** purpose, you will be **held / holding** liable for any costs.

14. When I worked last summer, I **had to / must** leave the apartment at seven o'clock every morning, and I often didn't **arrive / get** home until seven or eight **at / in** the evening.

15. When I arrived in the city I **made / spent** several days looking **after / for** somewhere to live, and **eventually / finally** found a nice apartment by the river.

16. I **hope / wish** I had more money. If I did, I **will / would** be able to buy a new computer, and get rid of this slow old thing that I've had **for / since** ages.

17. I moved here **at / in** April last year, and it's March now, so next month I'll **be / have been** here for exactly **a / one** year.

18. Last night, Ron asked me **about / for** $10 so that he **can / could** buy pizza, but I refused **lending / to lend** him anything.

Children and the family

Exercise 1

Complete definitions 1 – 15 with words and phrases from the box. There are some that you do not need.

adolescence	adolescent	adopt	authoritarian	birth rate	bring up	
dependent	divorced	extended family	family life	formative years		foster
foster child	foster family	freedom	infancy	infant	juvenile	
juvenile delinquency	lenient	minor (noun)	nuclear family		nurture	
over-protective	protective	raise	rebellious	relationship		relatives
responsible	separated	siblings	single parent	single-parent family		strict
supervision	running wild	teenager	upbringing	well-adjusted		

1. .... is the period in someone's life when they change from being a child to being a young adult. A boy or a girl who is at this stage in their life is called an ....

2. A .... is someone who has not reached the age at which they are legally an adult.

3. Your brothers and sisters are sometimes referred to as your ....

4. A couple (for example, a husband and wife) who are .... no longer live together. If a married couple get ...., their marriage is legally ended.

5. A .... is a family that looks after someone else's child in their own home for a period of time. A child who lives with this family is called a .... The verb is ....

6. A .... is a formal word for a young person, and can also be used as a word for a young person who has committed a crime.

7. A .... child is one who is mentally strong and able to deal with problems without becoming upset. A child who is badly behaved and refuses to obey his / her parents, teachers, etc., can be described as ....

8. Your .... are those in your life when your character and beliefs are most strongly influenced.

9. If you bring someone else's child into your family and legally make him or her your own child, we say that you .... him / her.

10. A .... is a child between the ages of 13 and 19.

11. An .... is a baby or very young child. This period in a child's life is called ....

12. .... and .... both mean the same thing: to take care of children while they are growing up.

13. An .... is a family group that includes grandparents, aunts, uncles, etc. A .... is a family unit consisting of a mother, a father and their children.

14. A .... or .... parent is one who makes their children follow rules and behave in a very 'correct' way. The opposite of this is ....

15. A .... is a child or other relative to whom you give food, money and a home. This word can also be an adjective.

<u>Exercise 2</u>

Use your dictionary to check the meanings of the other words and phrases in the box.

<u>Exercise 3</u>

Complete this case study with appropriate words and phrases from the box in Exercise 1. You may need to change the form of some of the words.

Bob's problems began during his (1) .... His parents got

(2) .... when he was young, and neither of his parents wanted to raise

him or his brother and sister, so he was (3) .... by a

(4) .... chosen by his parents' social worker. Unfortunately, his foster

father was a strict (5) .... and often beat him. Bob rebelled against this

strict (6) .... and by the time he was eight, he was already

(7) ...., stealing from stores and playing hooky. By the time he reached

(8) ...., sometime around his thirteenth birthday, he had already

appeared in court several times, charged with (9) .... The judge blamed

his foster parents, explaining that children needed (10) .... parents and

guardians who would look after them properly. The foster father objected to this, pointing out that Bob's

(11) .... – his two brothers and sister – were

(12) .... children who behaved at home and worked well at school.

This has raised some interesting questions about the modern family system. While it is true that parents

should not be too (13) .... with children by letting them do what they

want when they want, or be too (14) .... by sheltering them from the

realities of life, it is also true that they should not be too strict. It has also highlighted the disadvantages

of the modern (15) .... family, where the child has only its mother and

father to rely on (or the (16) .... in which the mother or father has to

struggle particularly hard to support their (17) ....). In fact, many believe

that we should return to traditional family values and the (18) .... family:

extensive research has shown that children from these families are generally better behaved and have a

getter chance of success in later life.

<u>Exercise 4</u>

Now try this essay. Use words and phrases from the vocabulary box in Exercise 1, and any other words or phrases that you think would be relevant.

Some people believe that children nowadays have too much freedom. Others believe that children are protected too much by their parents. Which of these statements do you agree with? Use specific reasons and examples to support your decision.

Exercise 1

Complete definitions 1 – 14 with words and phrases from the box. You will not need all of them.

| acquire   class   course   day release   degree   discipline   doctorate
elementary (education)   elementary school   enroll   exam   experience
faculty   fail   fees   grade   grades   grade school   graduate (noun)
graduate (verb)   graduate school   grant   higher degree   higher education
high school   junior high school   kindergarten   learn
learning resources center   lecture   lecturer   lesson   literacy
mature (student)   middle school   night class   numeracy   on line course
opportunity   pass   physical education   private school   professor
prospectus   public school   qualifications   quarter   resit (an exam)
resources   secondary (education)   semester   seminar
SAT® (Scholastic Aptitude Test)   sit / take (an exam)   skills   study   subject
syllabus   topic   tutor   tutorial   undergraduate |
| --- |

1. An .... is an educational course that you take at home, using your computer and the Internet. A .... is a lesson in the evening for people who work during the day. People who have a job might be given .... by their employer, which means that they can take a day off work about once a week to attend a course of study.

2. The .... is an examination that students in the United States must take before they can go to university.

3. A .... is a period of time in which students are taught a subject in school (also called a ....).

4. A .... is a talk given to a group of students at college or university about a particular .... The person who gives this talk is called a .... A .... is a meeting at which a group of students discuss something they are studying. A .... is a meeting at which one student, or a small group of students, discusses something that they are studying with their ....

5. .... is the ability to read and write. .... refers to basic skills in mathematics.

6. A .... is a small book that provides information about a university. Once a student who has read this book decides he / she would like to study there, he/she must .... (in other words, he / she puts his / her name on the official list of students).

7. A .... is a main department at a university. This word can also be used to refer to the teaching staff of a school, college, university, etc.

8. .... refers to sports and exercise that children do at school as a school subject.

9. A .... is a school that is funded by taxes.
A .... is a school where the parents of the children who attend it must pay ....

10. A .... is school for very young children (aged four or five), which prepares them for the first .... at school.
An .... is a school for the first six or eight years of a child's education. It is also known as a ....

11. A .... is a list of the main subjects in a course of study (sometimes called a curriculum).

12. A .... is a school for students between the ages of 12 and 14 or 15. It is also known as a .... From the age of 14 or 15, students attend a ....

13. A .... is one of two periods into which the school year is divided. A .... is one of four periods into which the school year is divided.

14. A .... is someone who has completed a course at school, college, or university. A .... is a college or university where students can study for a .... such as a Master's or PhD.

Exercise 2
Use your dictionary to check the meanings of the other words and phrases in the box.

Exercise 3
Complete this essay with appropriate words and phrases from the box in Exercise 1. You may need to change the form of some of the words.

'You are never too old to learn.' Do you agree with this statement?

Education is a long process that not only provides us with basic (1) .... such as (2) .... and (3) .... but is also essential in shaping our future lives. From the moment we enter (4) .... as five-year-olds, and as we progress through (5) .... and (6) .... education, we are laying the foundations for the life ahead of us. We must (7) .... ourselves to work hard so that we can (8) .... exams and gain the (9) .... we will need to secure a good job. We must also (10) .... valuable life skills so that we can fit in and work with those around us. And of course (11) .... helps us to develop our bodies and stay fit and healthy.

For most people, this process ends when they are in their mid-to-late teens and they (12) .... from high school. For others, however, it is the beginning of a lifetime of learning. After they finish school, many progress to (13) .... education where they will work towards a (14) .... in a chosen (15) .... at university. After that, they may work for a while before opting to study at a (16) .... for a Master's degree, or a (17) .... Alternatively, they may choose to attend a (18) .... after work or, if they have a sympathetic employer, obtain (19) .... so that they can study during the week. And if they live a long way from a college or university, they might follow an (20) .... using the Internet. In fact, it is largely due to the proliferation of computers that many people, who have not been near a school for many years, have started to study again and can proudly class themselves as (21) .... students.

We live in a fascinating and constantly changing world, and we must continually learn and acquire new knowledge if we are to adapt and keep up with changing events. Our schooldays are just the beginning of this process, and we should make the best of every (22) .... to develop ourselves, whether we are 18 or 80. You are, indeed, never too old to learn.

Exercise 4
Now try this essay. Use words and phrases from the vocabulary box in Exercise 1, and any other words or phrases that you think would be relevant.

Do you agree with this statement: 'The most important things in life are not learnt at school or college'? Use examples and details in your answer.

Food and diet

Exercise 1

Complete definitions and sentences 1 – 12 with words and phrases from the box. You will not need all of them.

allergy   allergic   anorexia   balanced diet   bulimia   calcium   calories carbohydrates   cholesterol   consume   consumption   diabetes diet (noun + verb)   eating disorder   exercise   fast food   fat   fat farm fiber   food groups   food Intolerance   food poisoning   free range   fresh genetically modified (GM)   harvest   health food   heart disease   junk food listeria   malnutrition   malnourished   minerals   monounsaturated   nutrition nutritious   obese   obesity   organic   overweight   processed   protein salmonella   saturated   scarce   scarcity   shortages   underweight vegan   veganism   vegetarian   vegetarianism   vitamins

1. .... is the part of fruit, vegetables, and grains that your body cannot digest, and helps food to pass through your body. .... is the oil found in food, and there are three main types of this: ...., polyunsaturated, and ....

2. .... are units used for measuring how much energy you get from food. .... is a substance found in food such as eggs, milk, and meat that people need in order to grow and be healthy. .... is a white chemical element that is an important part of bones and teeth, and is found in food products such as eggs, milk, and cheese. .... are found in foods such as sugar, bread, and potatoes, and supply your body with heat and energy.

3. People who weigh more than they should often go on a .... to help them lose weight. Some of them may go to a ...., an informal expression for a place where people can go to try to lose weight by eating in a healthy way and doing lots of ....

4. .... food is food which is produced without using artificial chemicals. .... food is food produced from animals which are allowed to move around and feed naturally. .... food is food that has been produced from a plant or animal that has had its gene structure changed in order to make it more productive or resistant to disease.

5. People who eat too much, or who don't eat enough (often because they think they look fat), suffer from a medical condition known generally as an .... Examples of this include .... and ....

6. A .... is someone who doesn't eat meat.
    A .... is someone who doesn't eat meat or other products derived from animals (including cheese and milk).

7. .... is food that is made very quickly, especially food like burgers and pizzas that you can take away. It is sometimes called ...., because it is often not very healthy or ....

8. Someone who is heavier than they should be is .... If they are a *lot* heavier than they should be, they are .... The noun is .... This can result in ...., cancer, ..., and many other serious illnesses.

9. E-coli, ..., and .... are three kinds of ....

10. Meat, vegetables, and dairy products are three of the main ....

11. If you eat a ...., you eat the correct amounts of the right sorts of food; you do not eat too much of one particular sort of food.

12.   People who have a .... are unable to eat certain kinds of food because it has a negative effect on them (although it may not affect them seriously). People with an .... to certain kinds of food must avoid them, as the effects may be much more serious (for example, if someone who is .... to peanuts eats something with peanuts in, it might kill them).

Exercise 2
Use your dictionary to check the meanings of the other words and phrases in the box.

Exercise 3
Complete this essay with appropriate words and phrases from the box in Exercise 1. You may need to change the form of some of the words.

Children love eating (1) ...., but burgers, chicken nuggets and other

heavily (2) .... food products not only contain a large number of

unhealthy chemicals and other additives, but also lack the essential (3) ....

and (4) .... that a child needs. In addition, they also contain a lot of

(5) .... and (6) ....which, if eaten in

quantity, can result in childhood (7) .... (in fact, a recent survey suggests

that 39% of 8 – 15 year-olds are seriously overweight).

Many children end up (8) ...., since they eat too much of the wrong sort

of food. In fact, in many parts of the developed world, a lot of children show similar symptoms to those

in poorer developing countries, where food (9) .... cause thousands of

deaths from starvation, especially in the wake of natural disasters which ruin crops and in some cases

totally destroy the annual (10) .... Furthermore, the large amounts of

(11) .... in animal and dairy products (a common feature of fast food)

are believed to be partly responsible for increased cases of heart disease in young people, a recent

phenomenon that is causing great concern.

It is therefore important children learn the benefits of eating a (12) ....,

as it is essential they consume sufficient quantities of the different food groups. They should be

encouraged to eat more (13) .... fruit and vegetables, and also more

food that is high in (14) .... They should still be allowed the occasional

burger or pizza, but these should be seen as an occasional treat rather than forming the main part of

their diet.

Exercise 4
Now try this essay. Use words and phrases from the vocabulary box in Exercise 1, and any other words or phrases that you think would be relevant.

'If food tastes good, it's probably bad for you'. How far do you agree with this statement? Use specific reasons and examples to support your opinion.

The media

Exercise 1

Complete sentences and definitions 1 – 12 with words and phrases from the box. You will not need all of them.

airtime audience broadcast broadsheet censor censorship channel check book journalism circulation current affairs coverage documentary download dumbing down editor entertainment exploit feature freedom of the press gutter press honest information informed Internet invasion of privacy journalism journalist libel libelous log on mass media media circus media event media tycoon news on line paparazzi the press program read between the lines readership reality TV reporter restriction slander slanderous tabloid tabloid TV unscrupulous Web site

1. .... is the crime of saying something about someone that is not true and is likely to damage their reputation (the adjective is ....) . ... is the illegal act of writing things about someone that are not true (the adjective is ....).

2. If you ...., you guess something that is not expressed directly (for example, if a newspaper reports a story, it might not tell you the truth or give you all the information you want, so you try to guess what that information is).

3. .... is an occasion when someone finds out or uses information about your private life.

4. A .... is a newspaper that is printed on large sheets of paper, and usually contains serious news. A .... is a newspaper that is printed on smaller sheets of paper and generally contains stories about famous people (papers like these are sometimes referred to as the ...., because many of the stories are either untrue, or are about sex and crime). .... refers to television programs that are intended to be shocking or exciting.

5. If a media company is accused of .... its stories or programs, it means that it presents these stories or programs in a simple and attractive way without giving many details.

6. A .... is someone who writes news reports for newspapers, television, etc. A .... often does the same thing, and then tells people the news himself / herself (for example, by appearing on a television program).

7. The process of removing parts of books, films, letters, etc., that are considered unsuitable for moral, religious or political reasons is called ....

8. A .... is someone who owns and controls several different newspapers, television stations, etc., and is very rich as a result.

9. .... programs are television programs in which ordinary people are put into artificially-created environments and situations in order to entertain people (the most famous example is *Big Brother*).

10. A .... is a radio or television program that deals with real people, events, places, etc., and is designed to inform people about different things. A .... program is one that deals mainly with political, social, and economic events that are happening now.

11. .... is the practice of paying people a lot of money for information that can be used in newspaper stories, especially stories about crime or famous people.

12. .... refers to the amount of time given to someone or something in a radio or television broadcast. .... refers to the amount of attention that television, radio, and newspapers give to something, or to the way in which something is reported. A newspaper's .... is the group or number of people who read that newspaper.

Exercise 2

Use your dictionary to check the meanings of the other words and phrases in the box.

Exercise 3

Complete this essay with appropriate words and phrases from the box in Exercise 1. You may need to change the form of some of the words.

> The media plays a valuable role in keeping us informed and entertained. However, many people believe it has too much power and freedom. Do you agree?
>
> Barely a hundred years ago, if we wanted to stay (1) .... about what was going on in the world, we had to rely on word of mouth or, at best, newspapers. But because communication technology was very basic, the news we received was often days or weeks old.
>
> We still have newspapers, of course, but they have changed almost beyond recognition. Whether we choose to read the (2) .... with their quality (3) .... of news and other (4) .... by top (5) .... and acclaimed (6) .... or if we prefer the popular (7) .... with their lively gossip and colorful stories, we are exposed to a wealth of information barely conceivable at the beginning of the last century.
>
> We also have television and radio. News (8) .... let us know about world events practically as they happen, while sitcoms, chat shows, and (9) ...., etc., keep us entertained and informed. And there is also the (10) .... where we can access information from millions of (11) .... around the world which we can then (12) .... onto our own computers.
>
> However, these forms of (13) .... and (14) .... (or 'infotainment' as they are now sometimes collectively called) have their negative side. Famous personalities frequently accuse the (15) .... (and sometimes even respectable papers) of (16) .... by camera-wielding (17) .... who are determined to get a picture or a story regardless of who they upset. Newspapers are often accused of (18) .... by angry politicians who hate reading damaging lies about themselves, and there are frequent accusations of (19) ...., with (20) .... newspapers paying people vast sums of money to tell them about the crime they committed or what their famous neighbor has been up to. Of course, it is not just the papers which are to blame. Sex and violence are increasing on the television, and many complain that there is increased (21) .... of news and current affairs programs, with major stories being presented in a simple and attractive way, but with very little detail. Others argue that too much time is being given to (22) .... shows, in which ordinary people are put into artificially created environments and situations for our entertainment. Meanwhile, anyone with a computer can go (23) .... to find undesirable material placed there by equally undesirable people.
>
> Some people argue that the government should impose stricter (24) .... to prevent such things happening. But others argue that (25) .... and media is the keystone of a free country. Personally, I take the view that while the media may occasionally abuse its position of power, the benefits greatly outweigh the disadvantages. Our lives would be much emptier without the wealth of information available to us today, and perhaps we are better people as a result.

Exercise 4

Now try this essay. Use words and expressions from the box in Exercise 1, and any other words or expressions that you think would be relevant.

What are the qualities or features of a good newspaper, current affairs television program, or news Web site? Use specific details and examples to explain your answer.

Money and finance

Exercise 1

Complete sentences and paragraphs 1 – 20 with a word or phrase from the box. In each case, the word / phrase you need is connected in some way with the word in **bold** in the same sentence / paragraph (for example, it might have a similar meaning, it might be an opposite, or it might be a word that is sometimes confused with that word). In some cases you might need to change the form of the word in the box.

---

balance   bank   bankrupt   bargain   bill   borrow   broke   cash
check   cost of living   credit card   credit   debt   debit   deposit
discount   distribution of wealth   dividends   economical   economize
exorbitant   expenditure   extravagant   frugal   income   income tax
inflation   inherit   insolvent   interest   in the black   in the red   invest
investment   invoice   lend   loan   loss   market   mortgage   on credit
overcharged   overdraft   overpriced   pension   priceless   profit   receipt
reduction   refund   salary   save   savings and loan association   shares
statement   stocks   tax / rent (etc.) rebate   undercharged
unemployment / housing / child (etc.) welfare   wage   wealthy   welfare
withdraw   worthless

---

1.   **Income** is the money you receive (your *wage* or *salary* is part of your income), and
      .... refers to the money you spend.

2.   If you **lend** money, you let someone use your money for a certain period of time. If you
      .... money, you take someone's money for a short time, and then
      you pay it back.

3   A **discount** is the percentage by which a full price is reduced in a store.
      A .... is money paid back to a customer when, for example, they
      return something to a store.

4.   If a person or company is **insolvent**, they have lost all their money. If a person or company is
      ...., they have lost all their money, have then borrowed a lot, and
      cannot pay it back.

5.   A bank **statement** is a detailed written document from a bank showing how much money has gone
      into and come out of a bank account. A .... is the amount of
      money you have in your bank account.

6.   If your bank account is **in the red**, the amount of money you have spent is greater than the money
      you have made, and so you have less than $0 in your bank account. If your account is
      ...., you have some money in your bank account.

7.   An **invoice** is a note, or *bill*, sent to you to ask for payment for goods or services, and a
      .... is a note (from a store, for example) which shows how much
      you have paid for something.

8.   When you make a **profit**, you gain money from selling something which is more than the money
      you paid for it. When you make a ...., you have spent money which
      you have not gotten back.

9.   Something which is **overpriced** is too expensive. Something which is ....
      costs much more than its true value.

10. If you **save** money, you keep it so that you can use it later. If you .... money, you put it into property, stocks, etc., so that it will increase in value.

11. A **wage** and a .... are both money you receive for doing a job, but the first is usually paid *daily* or *weekly* and the second is usually paid *monthly*.

12. A **worthless** object is something which has no value. A .... object is an extremely valuable object.

13. If you **deposit** money in a bank account, you put money into your account. If you .... money, you take it out of your account.

14. If you have been **undercharged**, you have paid less than you should have for goods or services. If you have been ...., you have paid too much.

15. **Extravagant** describes someone who spends a lot of money. .... describes someone who is careful with money.

16. A **bill** is a piece of paper showing the amount of money that you have to pay for goods or services. A .... is the same thing, but shows what you have to pay after a meal in a restaurant.

17. When a bank account is **credited** with money, money is put into the account. When a bank account is ...., money is taken out.

18. A **bank** is a business which holds money for its clients, and deals with money generally. A .... is similar, but is usually used by people who want to save money, or to borrow money to buy a house.

19. A **loan** is money that you borrow from a bank to buy something. A .... is similar, but in this case the money is only used to buy property.

20. A **loan** is money that you borrow from a bank, where a formal arrangement has been made with the bank to borrow it. An .... is the amount of money that you take out of your bank account, which is more than there is in your account. It is usually done without making a formal arrangement with your bank.

Exercise 2

Use your dictionary to check the meanings of the other words and phrases in the box. Note that many of them can have more than one grammatical function without changing their form (for example, *balance* can be a noun *and* a verb). Also note that some of the words can have more than one meaning (for example, a *bill* is a banknote, and it is also a piece of paper showing you how much you have to pay for a product or service).

Exercise 3

Complete this conversation with appropriate words and phrases from the box in Exercise 1. You may need to change the form of some of the words.

Financial advice from a father to a son

In the play *Hamlet* by William Shakespeare, a father gives his son some financial advice. 'Neither a borrower nor a lender be', he says. He is trying to tell his son that he should never (1) .... money from anyone because it will make it difficult for him to manage his finances. Likewise he should never give a financial (2) .... to a friend because he will probably never see the money again, and will probably lose his friend as well.

The play was written over four hundred years ago, but today many parents would give similar advice to their children. Imagine the conversation they would have now:

Jim: Right, Dad, I'm off to college now.

Dad: All right, son, but let me give you some sound financial advice before you go.

Jim: Oh come on, Dad…

Dad: Now listen, this is important. The first thing you should do is to make sure you balance your
          (3) .... – the money you receive from me and Mom – and your
          (4) .... – the money you spend. If you spend too much, you will end
          up with an (5) .... at the bank. Don't expect me to pay it for you.

Jim: But it's so difficult. Things are so expensive, and the (6) .... goes up
          all the time. (7) .... is running at about 8%.

Dad: 8.2% to be exact. But you should try to (8) .... Avoid expensive
          stores and restaurants. Also, put your money in a good local (9) ....
          account . They offer a much higher rate of (10) .... than banks.
          Also, avoid buying things (11) ....

Jim: Why?

Dad: Because some stores charge you an (12) .... amount of money to buy
          things over a period of time. It's much better to (13) .... a little bit of
          money each week so that when you see something you want, you can buy it outright. Try to wait for
          the sales, when stores offer huge (14) .... and you can pick up a
          (15) .... And try to get a (16) ....

Jim: How do I do that?

Dad: Easy. When you buy something, ask the shop if they'll lower the price by, say, 5 or 10%. You'd be
          surprised how many will say, 'Sure, ok'.

Jim: I can't imagine that working in Macy's, but I'll give it a go. Anything else you think I should know?

Dad: Yes. When you eventually get a job and are earning a good salary, try to
          (17) .... the money in a good company. Buy
          (18) .... in government organizations or
          (19) .... in private companies. I know an accountant who can give
          you some good advice, if you like.

Jim: OK, Dad, I've heard enough. Thanks for the advice. It's been (20) ....

Dad: Well, it's true what they say: there are some things that money just can't buy.

Exercise 4

Now try this essay. Use words and phrases from the box in Exercise 1, and any other words or phrases that you think would be relevant.

Some people say that 'Money makes the world go round'; others say that 'Money is the root of all evil'. Which of these do you agree with? Use examples and details in your answer.

Nature and the environment

Replace the words and phrases in **bold** in sentences 1 – 15 with one of those from the box. You will not need all of the words and phrases from the box.

acid rain   activists   animal rights   battery farming   biodegradable packaging biodiversity   biofuels   breeding   (in) captivity   CFC gases   climatic change conservation   conserve   conservation program   contaminated   deforestation degradation   desertification   eco-friendly   ecological   ecology   ecosystem emissions   endangered species   environmentalists   environmentally friendly erosion   extinct   fossil fuels   fumes   genetically modified   green belt global warming   greenhouse effect   greenhouse gases   intensive farming natural behavior   natural resources   organic   organic farming ozone-friendly   ozone layer   poaching   pollute   (air) pollution   rare breeds rainforest   recycle   recycling   renewable / sustainable energy   research solar power   tidal energy   toxic waste   unleaded gas   wildlife management

1. In some countries, building is restricted or completely banned in the **area of farmland or woods and parks which surround a community**. ....

2. More and more companies are using **boxes, cartons, and cans which can easily be decomposed by organisms such as bacteria, or by sunlight, sea, water, etc.**, for their products. ....

3. The burning of some fuels creates **carbon dioxide, carbon monoxide, sulfur dioxide, and methane** which rise into the atmosphere. ....

4. Farmers have cleared acres of **thick wooded land in tropical regions where the precipitation is very high** to provide pasture for their cattle. ....

5. Planting trees and bushes can provide some protection from the **gradual wearing away** of soil. ....

6. We should all try to **process waste material so that it can be used again**. ....

7. Many shops now sell fruit and vegetables which are **cultivated naturally, without using any chemical fertilizers or pesticides**. ....

8. This bread is made from wheat which has been **altered at a molecular level so as to change certain characteristics which can be inherited**. ....

9. **The process of removing trees from an area of land** is destroying millions of acres of woodland every year. ....

10. **Polluted precipitation which kills trees** often falls a long distance from the source of the pollution. ....

11. Human activity has had a devastating effect on the **living things, both large and small**, in many parts of the word. ....

12. The **gases and other substances** which come from factories using oil, coal, and other **fuels which are the remains of plants and animals** can cause serious damage to the environment. ....

13. Don't drink that water. It's been **made dirty by something being added to it**. ....

14. Friends of the Earth, Greenpeace, and other **people concerned with protecting the environment** are holding an international summit in Geneva next month. ....

15. **The heating up of the earth's atmosphere by pollution** is threatening life as we know it. ....

Exercise 2
Use your dictionary to check the meanings of the other words and phrases in the box.

Exercise 3
Read this essay and complete the gaps with one of the words or phrases from the box in Exercise 1.

Environmental degradation is a major world problem. What causes this problem, and what can we do to prevent it?

There is no doubt that the environment is in trouble. Factories burn (1) ....
which produce (2) .... , and this kills trees. At the same time,
(3) .... rise into the air and contribute to
(4) .... which threatens to melt the polar ice cap. Meanwhile farmers clear
huge areas of (5) .... in places such as the Amazon to produce feeding
land for cattle or wood for building. Rivers and oceans are so heavily (6) ....
by industrial waste that it is no longer safe to go swimming. Cars pump out poisonous
(7) .... which we all have to breathe in.
(8) .... and overfishing are killing off millions of animals, including whales,
elephants, and other (9) .... In fact, all around us, all living things large and
small which comprise our finely balanced (10) .... are being systematically
destroyed by human greed and thoughtlessness.

There is a lot we can all do, however, to help prevent this. The easiest thing, of course, is to
(11) .... waste material such as paper and glass so that we can use it
again. We should also check that the things we buy from supermarkets are packaged in
(12) .... packaging which decomposes easily. At the same time, we
should make a conscious effort to avoid foods which are (13) .... (at least
until someone proves that they are safe both for us and for the environment). If you are truly committed
to protecting the environment, of course, you should only buy (14) ....
fruit and vegetables, safe in the knowledge that they have been naturally cultivated. Finally, of course, we
should buy a smaller car, as these cause less (15) .... than large sedans or
SUVs. Even better, we should try to make more use of public transportation.

Serious (16) .... however, do much more. They are aware of the global
issues involved and will actively involve themselves in (17) .... by making
sure our forests are kept safe for future generations. They will oppose activities which are harmful to
animals, such as (18) .... and they will campaign to keep the
(19) .... around our towns and cities free from new building.

We cannot all be as committed as them, but we can at least do our own little bit at a grass roots level.
We humans control our planet, but that doesn't mean we can do whatever we like with it.

Exercise 4
Now try this essay. Use words and phrases from Exercise 1, and any other words or phrases that you think would be relevant.

Some people think that the government should spend as much money as possible on protecting the environment. Others think this money should be spent on other things such as education and healthcare. Which one of these opinions do you agree with? Use specific reasons and details to support your answer.

On the road

Some of the words and phrases from the box below have been defined in sentences 1 – 16. In some cases, these definitions are <u>correct</u>, and in some they are <u>incorrect</u>. Decide which are which.

accelerate   accident   black spot   accident risk   auto theft   back out
brake   congestion   crosswalk   cut in (in a vehicle)   cycle lane   destination
dominate   drink-driving   driver   driver's license   driving test   expressway
fatalities   a fine   freeway   gas   highway   highway patrol   injuries
intersection   interstate   joyriding   mile   mobility   overtake   park and ride
pedestrian   pedestrian mall   pollution   public transport   pull in   pull over
road rage   road work   rush hour   safety island   sidewalk   to speed
speed limit   subsidized (e.g., public transport)   to tailgate   traffic light / signal
traffic calming   traffic circle / rotary   traffic-free zone   traffic jam
traffic school   transport strategy   turnpike

1. **Rush hour** is the time of day when there are not many vehicles on the road because most people are at home.   *Correct / Incorrect*

2. If a service such as public transportation is **subsidized**, all of its running costs are paid for by the government or a local authority.   *Correct / Incorrect*

3. A **traffic school** is a school for people who want to learn to drive a motor vehicle.
    Correct / Incorrect

4. An **expressway** is a wide road (usually in a city) where people can drive quickly, and is the US equivalent of a British *dual carriageway*.   *Correct / Incorrect*

5. **Road rage** is anger or violent behavior by one driver towards another driver.   *Correct / Incorrect*

6. **Traffic calming** measures are fines and other penalties imposed by the police on bad or dangerous drivers.   *Correct / Incorrect*

7. In the United States, the **interstate** is part of the national public transportation system (including trains and buses) which people use to travel around the country.   *Correct / Incorrect*

8. Someone who has been accused of **joyriding** has stolen a car in order to drive it for pleasure, usually in a dangerous way.   *Correct / Incorrect*

9. A **turnpike** is a main road in the eastern part of the United States that drivers must pay to use.
    Correct / Incorrect

10. Someone who **backs out** in a vehicle drives it very quickly and dangerously, usually in a busy or built-up area.   *Correct / Incorrect*

11. A **cycle lane** is a part of the road that is set aside for people on bicycles, and which may not be used by drivers of motor vehicles.   *Correct / Incorrect*

12. A **traffic-free zone** is a main road between major towns and cities that drivers do not have to pay to use.   *Correct / Incorrect*

13. **Fatalities** (in this context) refers to people who are injured in accidents on the road.
    Correct / Incorrect

14. A **black spot** is a place on a road where a lot of car accidents happen.   *Correct / Incorrect*

15. A **mile** is a measure of distance equivalent to 1.609 kilometers.   *Correct / Incorrect*

16. A **sidewalk** is a part of the road in a town or city where drivers can park their vehicle.
    Correct / Incorrect

Exercise 2
Use your dictionary to check the meanings of the other words and phrases in the box.

Exercise 3
Complete this article with appropriate words and phrases from the box in Exercise 1. You may need to change the form of some of the words.

(1) .... and (2) .... on our roads are increasing from year to year: last year, 2,827 people were killed and almost 300,000 hurt in traffic-related accidents in the state. Most of these were caused by drivers (3) .... in built-up areas, where many seem to disregard the 30mph (4) ...., or (5) ...., especially around July 4th and Thanksgiving, when more alcohol is consumed than at any other time of the year. In many cases, it is (6) .... who are the victims, knocked down as they are walking across the street at (7) .... by drivers who seem to have forgotten that a red (8) .... means 'Stop'.

But these innocent victims, together with the help of the highway patrol and local safety groups, are fighting back. In New Stockholm, a city plagued by (9) .... and (10) .... caused by traffic, and a notorious accident (11) .... for pedestrians and cyclists, the city council has recently implemented its new (12) ...., which has improved the flow of traffic to the benefit of those on foot or on two wheels. (13) .... measures such as speed bumps have slowed traffic down. (14) .... schemes have helped reduce the number of cars in the city, as office workers and shoppers leave their cars outside the city and bus in instead. Lincoln Street, the main shopping thoroughfare, has been designated a (15) ...., closed to all vehicles during the day. There are more (16) .... on main routes into the city, making it safer for the huge number of students and residents who rely on bicycles to get around. And (17) .... public transportation has helped to keep down the cost of using buses. Meanwhile, the police and the courts are coming down hard on drivers who misuse the roads, handing down large (18) .... or even jail sentences to selfish, inconsiderate drivers who believe it is their right to (19) .... the roads; for these people, (20) .... is not offered as a softer alternative.

Exercise 4
Now try this essay. Use words and phrases from the box in Exercise 1, and any other words or phrases that you think would be relevant.

Do you agree or disagree with the following statement: 'It is time we all relied less on private motor vehicles to get around, and instead used other forms of transport'? Use specific examples and details to support your answer.

Science and technology

Exercise 1
Complete definitions 1 – 15 with words and phrases from the box. You will not need all of them.

---

analyze   bioclimatology   biology   breakthrough   cellphone   chemistry
computers   control   cryogenics   cybernetics   development   digital
discover   discovery   e-mail   experiment   genetic engineering
genetic fingerprinting   genetic modification   geneticist
information technology (IT)   innovation   Internet   invent   invention
life expectancy   microchip   modified   molecular biology
nuclear engineering   physics   research   safeguard   scientist   technocrat
technologist   technophile   technophobe

---

1.   .... is the practice or science of changing the genes of a living thing, especially in order to make it more suitable for a particular purpose.

2.   A .... is a rule, law, or plan that protects people or something from harm or problems.

3.   .... is the study of living things.

4.   A .... is someone who does not like, trust or want to use technology, especially computers.

5.   A .... is a discovery or achievement that comes after a lot of hard work.

6.   .... is the study or use of computers and electronic systems for storing and using information.

7.   If something is ...., it is changed slightly in order to improve it.

8.   A .... is a scientist who studies or works in genetics.

9.   .... is the use of technology to make copies of natural things (for example, artificial body parts).

10. A .... is a scientist or other technical expert with a high position in industry or government.

11. .... is the detailed study of something in order to discover new facts.

12. .... is the science that studies the effects of low temperatures, especially the use of low temperatures for preserving the bodies of dead people.

13. An .... is a scientific test to find out what happens to someone or something in particular conditions.

14. .... is the length of time that someone is likely to live.

15. .... is the invention or use of new ideas, methods, equipment, etc.

Exercise 2
Use your dictionary to check the meanings of the other words and phrases in the box.

Exercise 3
Complete this essay with appropriate words and phrases from the box in Exercise 1. You may need to change the form of some of the words.

'Science and technology have come a long way in the last 60 years, and our lives have become better as a result.' Do you agree with this statement?

In scientific and technological terms, the twentieth century saw more changes than in the previous five hundred years. Penicillin was (1) .... and used to treat infections that would have once been fatal, and there were many other remarkable advances in medicine that helped to increase our average (2) .... way beyond that of our ancestors. Incredible (3) .... such as television changed the way we now spend our leisure hours. Perhaps the most important (4) .... , however, was the microchip. Nobody could have imagined, when it was first (5) .... , that within a matter of years, this tiny piece of silicon and circuitry would be found in almost every household object from the kettle to the camcorder. And nobody could have predicted the sudden proliferation of computers that would completely change our lives, allowing us to access information from the other side of the world via the (6) .... or send messages around the world by (7) .... at the touch of a button. Meanwhile, (8) .... into other aspects of information technology made it easier and cheaper for us to talk to friends and relations around the world. Good news for (9) .... who love modern technology, bad news for the (10) .... who would have preferred to hide from these modern miracles.

But everything has a price. The development of (11) .... led to mass automation in factories, which in turn led to millions losing their jobs. The genius of Einstein led to the horrors of the atomic bomb and the dangerous uncertainties of (12) .... (we often hear of accidents and mishaps at nuclear power stations around the world, where (13) .... to prevent accidents were inadequate). The relatively new science of (14) .... has been seen as a major step forward, but putting modified foods onto the market before scientists had properly (15) .... them was perhaps one of the most irresponsible decisions of the late twentieth and early twenty-first century. Meanwhile, pharmaceutical and cosmetic companies continue to (16) .... on animals, a move that many consider to be cruel and unnecessary.

Of course we all rely on modern science and technology to improve our lives. However, we need to make sure that we (17) .... it rather than the other way round.

Exercise 4
Now try this essay. Use words and phrases from the box in Exercise 1, and any other words or phrases that you think would be relevant.

What, in your opinion, has been the single most important scientific or technological development of the last 50 years? Use specific reasons and details to support your answer.

Town and country

Exercise 1

Complete sentences 1 – 12 with a word or phrase from the box. Then take the letter indicated at the end of each sentence, and write it in the grid that follows the sentences. If you do this correctly, you will 'find' another word which means *showing the influence of many different countries and cultures*.

agriculture   amenities   apartment block   arable land   atmosphere to breed crime   building sites   Central Business District (CBD)   commute commuter   commuter belt   congestion   construction   cost of living crops   crowded   cultivation   cultural events   depopulation   development drug abuse   employment   environment   fields   green belt   industry infrastructure   housing project   inner city   lively   mall / shopping mall melting pot   metropolis   migration   nature   nightlife   outskirts peaceful   peak period   pedestrian precinct   pollution   population population explosion   poverty   productive land   property prices   prospects resident   residential area   rural   rush hour   slum   street crime   stressful suburbs   unemployment   urban   urban lifestyle   urban sprawl

1.   If the town in which you live offers you good ...., it offers you the chance for success, especially in a job or career. (*Write the 7th letter of this word in the grid*)

2.   A .... is a big city, especially one that is busy and exciting. (*Write the 5th letter of this word in the grid*)

3.   An .... is the set of systems within a place or organization that affects how well it operates (for example, a public transport system or road system). (*Write the 6th letter of this word in the grid*)

4.   A .... is someone who travels regularly to and from work. (*Write the 3rd letter of this word in the grid*)

5.   The .... of a town or city are the areas that are furthest away from the center. (*Write the 1st letter of this word in the grid*)

6.   .... is a situation in which many people leave a place in order to live somewhere else, leaving very few people living there. (*Write the 3rd letter of this word in the grid*)

7.   .... occurs when there are a lot of vehicles on the road, and as a result the traffic moves very slowly. (*Write the 2nd letter of this word in the grid below*)

8.   If a town or city is described as a ...., it has people of many different races, religions, cultures, etc., living together. (*2 words: Write the 3rd letter of the 1st word in the grid*)

9.   .... refers to the movement of people from one place to another (often from one part of a country to another, or from one country to another country). (*Write the 2nd letter of this word in the grid*)

10.   If a situation, place, etc., is ...., it causes a lot of pressure and makes people worry. (*Write the 2nd letter of this word in the grid*)

11.   .... is an adjective relating to towns and cities. (*Write the 4th letter of this word in the grid*)

12.   A town's .... are the things that make it comfortable and pleasant to live in (for example, parks, theaters, stores, etc.). (*Write the 4th letter of this word in the grid*)

Sentence number:	1	2	3	4	5	6	7	8	9	10	11	12
Letter:												

Exercise 2
Use your dictionary to check the meanings of the other words and phrases in the box.

Exercise 3
Complete this essay with appropriate words and phrases from Exercise 1. You may need to change the form of some of the words, and one of the words you will need is the extra word you revealed by doing Exercise 1.

Describe a place where you live or have lived, outlining its good points and bad points.

For seven years I lived in Singapore, a (1) .... of over three million people. Like London, Paris, and New York, Singapore is a (2) .... city, with people from different parts of the world living and working together. I enjoyed the (3) .... lifestyle I led there, and made the most of the superb (4) ...., ranging from the excellent stores and shopping malls to some of the best restaurants in the world. In the evenings and at weekends there were always (5) ....: with such diverse attractions as classical western music, an exhibition of Malay art, or a Chinese opera in the street, it was difficult to get bored. Perhaps most impressive, however, was the remarkable transport (6) ...., with excellent roads, a swift and efficient bus service, and a state-of-the-art underground system which could whisk (7) .... from the suburbs straight into the heart of the city. This was particularly important, as the government imposed a charge on private cars entering the (8) .... during the morning and afternoon (9) .... in order to reduce (10) .... on the roads and (11) .... from the exhausts.

Of course, living in a city like this had its disadvantages as well. For a start, the (12) .... was very high – renting an apartment, for example, cost me almost half my salary. And as the city was continually expanding, there were a lot of (13) .... where new apartments were continually being built to deal with the (14) ...., a direct result of the government encouraging people to have more children.

Fortunately, Singapore doesn't suffer from problems that are common in many cities such as (15) ...., which is partly the result of the government imposing very severe penalties on anyone bringing narcotics into the country, so it is safe to walk the streets at night. In fact, the (16) .... housing estates there are probably the safest and most orderly in the world.

Singapore wouldn't be ideal for everyone, however, especially if you come from the countryside and are used to a (17) .... lifestyle. The traditional villages that were once common have disappeared as the residents there realized there were no (18) .... for their future and moved into new government housing in the city. Nowadays, there is very little (19) .... around the city, which means that Singapore imports almost all of its food. And despite a 'green' approach to city planning, the (20) .... which has eaten into the countryside has had a detrimental effect on the (21) ....

Exercise 4
Now try this essay. Use words and phrases from Exercise 1, and any other words or phrases that you think would be relevant.

Some people prefer to live in the countryside or in a small town. Others prefer to live in a big city. Which place would you prefer to live in? Use specific reasons and details to support your answer.

Travel

Look at the words and phrases in the box, then answer questions 1 – 16. Some of these questions ask you to explain what a word or phrase means, and some of them ask you to complete a sentence with the appropriate word(s) or phrase(s).

> acclimatize   alien   all-inclusive   business class
> check in (to a hotel or for a flight)   check out (of a hotel)   coach class
> consulate   cruise   culture shock   customs   deport   disembark   displaced
> economic migrants   ecotourism   embark   embassy   emigrate   emigration
> excursion   expatriate   first class   flight   gate   green card   illegal alien
> immigrant   immigration   independent traveler   internally displaced
> journey   long-haul   luggage   mass tourism   migrant   migrate
> package tour   package tourist   passport   persona non grata   refugee
> repatriate   safari   short-haul   tour operator   trafficking   travel agency
> travel agent   trip   UNHCR   visa   voyage   work permit

1. What does the expression *persona non grata* mean?

2. Complete this sentence: .... is the nervous or confused feeling that people sometimes get when they arrive in a place that is very different from the place they normally live.

3. What is the difference between a *travel agency* and a *tour operator*?

4. Complete this sentence: An .... is a short trip somewhere, usually for one day or part of a day.

5. Complete this sentence: A .... seat is the cheapest type of seat on a plane or train. The most expensive type of seat is called ....
    Between these two, there is ....

6. Would you be happy if the country that you were staying in *deported* you?

7. Complete this sentence: .... refers to the large numbers of people that travel for their vacation, usually over long distances.

8. What is the difference between a *package tourist* and an *independent traveler*?

9. Is a *refugee* the same as an *expatriate*?

10. What do you think the letters *UNHCR* stand for?

11. Complete this sentence: .... is the business of creating and selling holidays that give people the chance to learn about a natural environment, and which cause little damage to the environment itself.

12. If someone has been *repatriated*, what has happened to them?

13. What is a *cruise*? What is a *safari*?

14. Why might someone want a *green card*?

15. If someone is *trafficking* something, are they doing something that is *legal* or something that is *illegal*?

16. Complete this sentence: A person who has been .... has been forced to move from one part of their country to another (often because of a war or other threatening situation).

Exercise 2
Read this essay and complete the gaps with one of the words or phrases from the box in Exercise 1.
You may need to change the form of some of the words.

'There are two types of traveler: those who do it because they *want* to, and those who do it because they *have* to' Discuss this statement, using specific examples.

Most of us have, at some point in our lives, experienced the joys of travel. We go to a
(1) .... to pick up some brochures, or look on the Internet for a cheap
holiday deal. We book a two-week (2) .... with flights and
accommodation included, (or if we are (3) .... , we make our own way
to the country and travel around from place to place with a rucksack on our back). We make sure we
have all the right currency, our passport and any (4) .... that are
necessary to get us into the country. We go to the airport and (5) ....
We strap ourselves into our tiny (6) .... aircraft seats and a few hours
later we (7) .... from the aircraft, strange new sights, smells and sounds
greeting us. Nowadays, it seems, the whole world goes on holiday at once: the age of
(8) .... is in full swing!

But for the great majority of people around the world, travel for them is done in the face of great
adversity and hardship. They never get to indulge in an (9) .... holiday in
a luxury hotel with all meals and drinks included. They never get to explore the lush Amazon rainforest or
the frozen wastes of the Arctic on an (10) .... holiday. For them, travel is
a matter of life and death. I refer, of course, to all the (11) .... escaping
from danger in their own countries, or the (12) .... moved from one part
of their country to another by an uncaring government, or (13) ....
forced to find a job and seek a living wherever they can.

Can you imagine anything worse than the misery these people must face? Let us not confuse them with
those (14) .... who choose to live in another country and often have nice
houses and high salaries. These people are simply desperate to survive. As well as losing their homes
because of war or natural disasters, they must come to terms with their new environment: for many, the
(15) .... can be too great. And while many countries with an open policy
on (16) .... will welcome them in with open arms, others will simply turn
them away. These people become (17) .... , unwanted and unwelcome.
Even if they manage to get into a country, they will often be (18) .... or
repatriated. Their future is uncertain.

Perhaps this is something we should all think about the next time we are
(19) .... to our five-star hotel by a palm-fringed beach or sitting in a bus
on an (20) .... to castle or other historical site in the countryside.

Exercise 3
Now try this essay. Use words and phrases from the box in Exercise 1, and any other words or phrases
that you think would be relevant.

What are the good things and bad things about traveling? Use specific examples to explain your answer.

Work

Look at the words and phrases in the box, and use some of them to answer questions 1 – 14. You may need to change the form of some of the words.

adverse working conditions   applicant   application form   be made redundant blue-collar worker   boss   candidate   commission   demanding   dismiss dismissal   downsize   employee   employer   fire   fixed income flexible working hours   freelance   full time   hire   homeworker   incentives incentive scheme   income   increment   interview   interviewee   interviewer job satisfaction   job security   manager   manual worker manufacturing industry   (on) leave   overtime   part-time   pension pension contributions   perks   profession   promotion   raise recruitment drive   repetitive strain injury (RSI)   resign   retire rewards and benefits   salary   self-employed   semi-skilled   service industry sick building syndrome   sickness benefit   skilled   a steady job   stress supervisor   unemployed   unemployment   union   unskilled unsociable hours   wage   (on) welfare   white-collar worker   workaholic

1. Replace the word in **bold** in this sentence with another word from the box which has a similar meaning: 'A lot of people wanted the job, but she was the best **candidate**'.

2. What is the difference between a *wage* and a *salary*?

3. Complete this sentence: .... is a painful condition of the muscles in the hands and the arms caused by doing the same movement many times (for example, using a computer over a long period of time).

4. Replace the word in **bold** in this sentence with another word from the box which has a similar, but less formal, meaning (you will need to change the form of the word): 'When he was caught stealing from the company, he was instantly **dismissed** ....'.

5. Complete this sentence: The word *raise* in the box is similar in meaning to .... (which is also in the box).

6. What is the difference between a *blue-collar worker* and a *white-collar worker*?

7. True or false?: When a company *downsizes* its work force, this means that it pays its workers less than before. ....

8. Complete this sentence: .... are extra payments or benefits that you get in your job (for example, free meals, health insurance, company car, etc.).

9. What do you think *sick building syndrome* is?

10. Complete this sentence: If you have ...., you have work which is reliable and will last for a long time.

11. True or false?: *retire* and *resign* have the same meaning. ....

12. Complete this sentence: Banks, hospitals, and hotels are examples of ....

13. Would you be happy if you had *adverse working conditions*?

14. Complete this sentence: A person who is .... is not permanently employed by one company, but sells their services to more than one company.

Exercise 2
Use your dictionary to check the meanings of the other words and phrases in the box.

Exercise 3
Complete this essay with appropriate words and phrases from the box in Exercise 1. You may need to change the form of some of the words.

'Some people live to work and others work to live. In most cases, this depends on the job they have and the conditions under which they are employed.' In your opinion, what are the elements that make a job worthwhile?

In answering this question, I would like to look first at the elements that combine to make a job *un*desirable. By avoiding such factors, potential (1) .... are more likely to find a job that is more worthwhile, and by doing so, hope to achieve happiness in their work.

First of all, it doesn't matter if you are an (2) .... worker cleaning the floor, a (3) .... (4) .... worker on a production line in one of the (5) .... , or a (6) .... worker in a bank, shop, or one of the other (7) ....: if you lack (8) ...., with the knowledge that you might lose your job at any time, you will never feel happy. Everybody would like a (9) .... in which he or she is guaranteed work. Nowadays, however, companies have a high turnover of staff, (10) .... new staff and (11) .... others on a weekly basis. Such companies are not popular with their workers. The same can be said of a job in which you are put under a lot of (12) .... and worry, a job which is so (13) .... that it takes over your life, a job where you work (14) .... and so never get to see your family or friends, or a physical job in which you do the same thing every day and end up with the industrial disease that is always in the papers nowadays – (15) ....

With all these negative factors, it would be difficult to believe that there are *any* elements that make a job worthwhile. Money is, of course, the prime motivator, and everybody wants a good (16) .... But of course that is not all. The chance of (17) ...., of being given a better position in a company, is a motivating factor. Likewise, (18) .... such as a free lunch or a company car, an (19) .... scheme to make you work hard such as a regular (20) .... above the rate of inflation, (21) .... in case you fall ill, and a company (22) .... scheme so that you have some money when you retire all combine to make a job worthwhile.

Unfortunately, it is not always easy to find all of these. There is, however, an alternative. Forget the office and the factory floor and become (23) ....instead. When you work for yourself, your future may not be all that secure. However, at least you will be happy.

Exercise 4
Now try this essay. Use words and phrases from the box in Exercise 1, and any other words or phrases that you think would be relevant.

'It is more important to have a job you enjoy doing than a job which pays well.' How far do you agree with this statement? Use specific reasons and examples to support your answer.

Mini topics

Friends and relations

<u>Exercise 1</u>
Complete the sentences with the most appropriate words and phrases from the box. In some cases, more than one answer is possible, and there are some words you do not need.

acquaintance   admire   amiable   a lot in common   bond   boss   brother close   employee   fallen out   family ties   friendship   kinship on good terms   related   relationship   respect   see eye to eye shared interests   siblings   sister   supportive

1. I have two ....: an older ....called Robert, and a younger ...., Louise.

2. I have ....with my friend Andy, and we have several ...., like football and photography.

3. My father and I don't always ....on everything, but there's a good ....between us and we've never .... with each other over anything.

4. I'm ....with my ...., Mrs Underhill. She treats me as a friend rather than an ...., and she's always very ....if I have problems at work.

5. I know Sally, but not particularly well. We like and ....each other, but we're not .... She's an .... rather than a friend.

6. Everyone likes Alice: she's a very ....person. She also looks a lot like me, but we're not ....in any way.

<u>Exercise 2</u>
Now answer these questions.

1. Choose the best word in bold to complete this sentence: Sue and I really like each other – there's really good **chemistry / biology / physics** between us.
2. True or false?: *bring up* a child and *raise* a child have the same meaning.
3. Rearrange the letters in bold to make an informal word for a friend: **uydbd**
4. True or false?: to *get on with* someone is the same as to *adore* someone.
5. Choose the best word to in bold to complete this sentence: I have a shared bedroom in the college dorm. My **colleague / classmate / room mate** is great fun.
6. What's the difference between a *nuclear family* and an *extended family*?
7. True or false?: a *relation* is the same as a *relative*.
8. Rearrange the letters in bold to make a formal word for a girlfriend or boyfriend: **rpnetar**
9. What does it mean when we describe two people as being *inseparable*?
10. Rearrange the letters in bold to make the opposite of a friend: **meyne**
11. True or false?: *spouse* is a formal word for a child.
12. Choose the best word to in bold to complete this sentence: My fourth grade form teacher Mr Wickham was a real **inspire / inspiration / inspiring** to me.

<u>Exercise 3</u>
Now try this essay. Use words and phrases from Exercises 1 and 2, and any other words or phrases that you think would be relevant.

Different people influence our lives in different ways. How? Illustrate your answer with specific examples.

Health and exercise

Exercise 1

Complete the sentences with the most appropriate words and phrases from the box. In some cases, more than one answer is possible, and there are some words you do not need.

active	aerobics	balanced diet	cut down	eating disorder	fall ill
fast food	fat	give up	go jogging	go swimming	health club
health problems	heart disease	in good shape	keep fit	lifestyle	
look after	obese	obesity	on a diet	overweight	put on weight
sedentary	skin problems	slim	take up	underweight	unhealthy

1. In order to stay.., you need to remain
    .... A simple way of doing this is to ....
    two or three times a week. You could also ....a competitive sport, like
    squash or tennis.

2. ....people often become ....,
    especially if they eat too much ...., or food that has a high sugar
    and ....content.

3. Sam looks really ....these days. He's
    ....in the last few months, and he has terrible
    .... It's time he started eating a ....
    instead of living on chips and candy all the time.

4. People often ask me how I stay so ....when I eat so much.
    Well, I have a busy ...., which helps, and I'm also a member of a
    local ...., where I go at the weekends to
    ....

5. My doctor told me that I didn't ....myself properly. He advised me to go
    .... so that I'd lose some weight, ... on
    fatty and sugary foods, and .... smoking altogether.

6. .... is becoming a major problem, especially among young people.
    They need to be aware that being .... can lead to serious
    .... such as diabetes and ....

Exercise 2

Now try this essay. Use words and phrases from Exercise 1, and any other words or phrases that you think would be relevant.

Too many young people these days are unhealthy and / or overweight. What advice would you give somebody who wanted to become fit and healthy?

Movies and the theater

<u>Exercise 1</u>

Complete the conversations with the most appropriate words and phrases from the box. In some cases, more than one answer is possible, and there are some words you do not need.

acting	actor	actress	atmosphere	audience	believable	big budget
box office	cast	characters	comedy	director	documentary	drama
entertaining	exciting	feel-good	frightening	funny	horror	musical
performance	play	plot	science fiction	screen	soundtrack	
special effects	stage	stars	storyline	terrifying	thriller	

1. **Tom:** I loved the music in that movie we saw the other week.
   Lisa: Which one?
   Tom: That .... movie. You know, the one about the alien invaders trashing Los Angeles.
   Lisa: Oh, that one. Yes, the music was good. I wonder if you can get the .... anywhere.

2. **John:** What did you do last night?
   Kelly: I watched a movie on TV called *What Happened to my Dog?*. It was supposed to be a ...., but it wasn't very .... In fact, I didn't laugh once. And the .... was terrible.

3. **Mike:** Who's your favorite ....?
   Don: Kiera Knightley.
   Mike: And your favorite ....?
   Don: Probably Clint Eastwood.
   Mike: I thought he was a ....
   Don: Well, he does both.

4. **Ian:** I saw a great .... movie the other night.
   Judy: Oh, I hate those. All those monsters and zombies and stuff. They're really .... I always have nightmares after watching them.
   Ian: This one was great. There wasn't much of a .... I mean, nothing really happened, you know? But the .... were fantastic. At times, it seemed like the monsters were about to come right out of the ....
   Judy: It sounds absolutely ....

5. **Brad:** What was the name of the .... you saw on Broadway at the weekend?
   Jenny: *Singing for your Supper*. Actually, it was a ....
   Brad: Was it any good?
   Jenny: Oh, fantastic. Really .... The songs were great, and the dance routines were amazing. And I've never seen such a professional .... They were fantastic, so professional.
   Brad: Anyone famous?
   Jenny: I don't think there were any big ...., but I recognized one or two familiar faces.

6.   **Clark:** What kind of movies do you like?

Jan: I like .... movies. You know, the sort where you leave the theater with a big smile on your face and a nice, warm feeling inside.

Clark: Me too. And that feeling you get when the .... all get really involved in the movie, you know, when they really relate to the .... in the story, and you get a great .... in the theater.

Exercise 2

Now try this essay. Use words and phrases from Exercise 1, and any other words or phrases that you think would be useful.

What kinds of movies do you enjoy watching, and why do you enjoy watching them? Use specific examples to explain your answer.

❖ ❖ ❖ ❖ ❖

Your home town

Exercise 1

Complete the sentences with the most appropriate words and phrases from the box. There are some you do not need.

amenities   busy   character   community spirit   demolished   environment
healthcare   historic   homelessness   housing projects   job opportunities
local customs   monuments   museum   neighborhood   neighbors   nightlife
parks   peaceful   pedestrianized   population   public transport   rejuvenated
renovated   rural   shopping mall   sports center   street crime
traffic congestion   unemployment   urban

What do I like about my home town?

1.   It has great .... There's always something to do in the evening.

2.   There's a real .... Everyone gets on well and works together to keep the town a pleasant place.

3.   It has a lot of .... There are some really interesting streets and buildings.

4.   The center of the town is ...., so you can walk the streets without worrying about the traffic.

5.   There's an excellent ....: it has tennis courts, a basketball court, a baseball field, and a large swimming pool.

6.   We've also got a really good .... The section on ancient Egyptian art is amazing.

7.   My .... I think I live in the nicest part of the town.

8.   My .... They're some of the nicest folks I know.

9.   There's a huge .... You can buy anything you like there.

10. .... facilities are excellent, so if you fall ill or have an accident, you know you're in good hands.

11. There are some beautiful .... where you can go to sunbathe, play a ball game, or just chill out with your friends.

12. There are plenty of other ...., like a huge library, theaters, hotels, lots of restaurants, and some great bars and cafés.

13. The town has plenty of .... You can always find work if you need it.

14. A lot of old buildings have been .... They look as good as they did when they were first built.

15. Some ugly 1960s buildings have been ...., and modern apartments built in their place.

16. Some areas of the town which were in decline have been .... Now they're really nice places to live or work.

17. There are some interesting .... buildings, including a fort that dates back to the War of Independence.

18. There's no .... You don't see people living on the streets.

19. There's almost no .... It's safe to go out at night without worrying about being attacked or robbed.

20. There's very little .... Cars and trucks can move freely and easily around the town.

21. The .... system is one of the best in the state. An excellent bus service and a new subway mean people can get in and out of the town center easily.

22. The .... is really clean, because the local council have imposed strict anti-pollution measures.

23. Because of all the trees and open green spaces, the town has a wonderful .... feel to it.

24. There are some interesting and unusual .... These include people throwing flowers at each other on Independence Day, and a race called 'Chasing the boundary', which goes back 200 years.

Exercise 2
Now try this essay. Use words and phrases from the box, and any other words or phrases that you think would be relevant.

You have been asked for some suggestions to make your home town a better place. What suggestions would you make, and why?

Learning languages

Exercise 1
Rearrange the letters in bold in sentences 1–18 to make words and phrases, then use the words and phrases to complete the crossword. Do not leave any spaces between words in the crossword.

1. I'm quite worried about my lack of **esgrpsro** in English.
2. I don't speak French well, but I manage to **etg yb** in the language when I go to France.
3. If you're not sure what a word means, you should look it up in a **ondaitiryc**
4. I speak English quite well, but I think I still have quite a strong Spanish **cetcan**.
5. I don't speak Malay, but on my last trip to Malaysia, I managed to **ikpc pu** a bit of the language.
6. My father is **iualngbli**. He speaks Russian and English perfectly.
7. One of the best ways of developing your English **abyulvocra** is to read as much as possible.
8. In my country, everyone learns English as a **ecdosn gnglaeua**.
9. My English isn't great. I'd say that I was **ecmpntoet** in the language, but no more.
10. I come from Brazil, so my **heotmr utgeon** is Portuguese.
11. I have quite a few problems with my English **ontiunprciano**. I find the combination of t and h particularly difficult.
12. When you are learning a language, it is important to **retpicac** using it as much as possible.
13. When you move to another country, you should learn about the local **uulrect** as well as learn the language.
14. Learning **margarm** is usually quite boring, but our teacher always makes it interesting and fun.
15. After working in Tokyo for 10 years, he spoke **elntuf** Japanese.
16. The main advantage of learning a language is that you can **uncoiatemcm** effectively with more people.
17. I always thought my German was quite good, until I tried using it for the first time with **ivneat** speakers!
18. In my opinion, learning a language is challenging but **warngrdie**.

Exercise 2

Now try this essay. Use words and phrases from the box, and any other words or phrases that you think would be useful.

What are the most effective ways of learning a foreign language? Illustrate your answer with specific examples.

Vocabulary record sheet

Photocopy this page as many times as you like, and use it to keep a record of new words, phrases, and expressions that you learn. Try to build up a personal vocabulary bank, and keep this in a file or folder with the words, etc., stored in alphabetical order. See the next page for a sample completed record sheet.

Word or phrase:	
Topic area(s) (if relevant):	
Definition(s):	
Translation or equivalent in my language:	
Other forms of this word (if relevant):	
Sample sentences:	
Other collocations:	
Related words, phrases, and expressions:	
Other information:	

You may photocopy this page

Sample vocabulary record sheet

Word or phrase:	*Reject (verb, regular, transitive) / rI'dzekt /*

Topic area(s) (if relevant):	*Refusing or disagreeing*

Definition(s):	*1. to not agree to an offer, proposal, or request.*
	2. to disagree with an idea, argument, or suggestion.
	3. to refuse to take something, maybe because it is damaged.
	4. to behave in an unkind way to someone who wants kindness or love.
	5. (of a human body) to have a bad reaction to an organ after a transplant.

Translation or equivalent in my language:	*rejeter / refuser*

Other forms of this word (if relevant):	*reject, rejection (noun)*
	'Reject' can also be used as a noun without changing its form when we are talking about something that is not accepted because it has not reached the necessary standard: 'The computer was cheap because it was a reject'.

Sample sentences:	*It is almost certain that our offer will be rejected.*
	The court rejected the defendant's argument.
	The company rejected the whole shipment.
	He claimed he had been rejected by his parents.
	His body rejected the kidney and he became seriously ill.

Other collocations:	*to reject categorically / decisively / firmly / flatly / out of hand / outright / totally / unanimously / vigorously.*
	With the exception of 'outright' and 'out of hand', these words can also come <u>before</u> the word 'reject'.

Related words, phrases, and expressions:	*refuse, decline, turn down, throw out, veto, dismiss, rebuff, shun, snub, take a rain check (idiom. 'Would you like to go for a meal tonight?' 'I'll take a rain check if that's ok with you')*

Other information:
The opposite of reject is accept. The opposite of rejection is acceptance.
Reject is often used with as + an adjective or adjective phrase:
'He rejected the idea as ridiculous'. 'She rejected my offer as being too expensive'.

Answer key

Addition, equation and conclusion (page 4)

Exercise 1

Addition:	and along with (this could also be equation) also as well as besides furthermore in addition moreover too what's more
Equation:	equally correspondingly in the same way likewise similarly
Conclusion:	in conclusion in brief thus to conclude to summarize to sum up briefly therefore we can conclude that

Exercise 2

1. Furthermore / Moreover / In addition / What's more (this is less formal than the other expressions)   **2.** As well as / Besides   **3.** Likewise / Similarly / In the same way (the verbs in both sentences – i.e., *respect* – are the same and refer to the same thing, so we can use a word of equation here)   **4.** As well as / Along with   **5.** In addition   **6.** Likewise / Similarly   **7.** Likewise / In the same way / Correspondingly   **8.** In brief   **9.** We can conclude that   **10.** Therefore (*To sum up, To conclude* and *To summarize* are usually used to conclude longer pieces of writing – e.g., at the end of an essay. *Thus* is slightly more formal than *therefore*, but has the same meaning)

Note: It is important that you are familiar with the way these words and phrases are used, including the other words in a sentence that they 'work' with. Use a dictionary to look up examples of these words and phrases, and keep a record of them to refer to the next time you use them.

American English (pages 5 – 7)

Across

2. intermission   **6.** over (in the context of repeating something completely only. In other contexts, *again* is used in the same way as it is used in British English)   **8.** mail   **9.** recognize (note that in British English, this word can be spelt *recognise* or *recognize*)*   **11.** theater*   **13.** underpass   **16.** gas   **18.** elevator   **20.** realtors   **24.** highway   **26.** raise   **27.** recess   **29.** guy   **30.** faculty**   **32.** fall   **35.** sedan   **36.** store   **37.** defense*   **38.** round-trip   **40.** alumnus   **41.** cellphone

Down

1. zip code   **3.** through   **4.** movies (*movie theater* is also used)   **5.** bill   **7.** labor*   **10.** gotten   **12.** apartments   **14.** travelers*   **15.** first   **17.** sidewalk   **19.** movie   **21.** freeway (*expressway* is also used)   **22.** this   **23.** dialog*   **25.** drugstore   **28.** subway   **31.** attorney (*lawyer* is also used)   **33.** eraser   **34.** vacation   **39.** bathroom

* Note the following spelling differences between British and American English:

- Words which usually end in *–ise* in British English end with *–ize* in American English (*recognize, realize, itemize*, etc.).
- Words which end with *–re* in British English usually end with *–er* in American English (*theater, center, liter*, etc.).
- Words which end with *–our* in British English normally end with *–or* in American English (*humor, labor, color*, etc.).
- Words which end with *–ogue* in British English normally end with just *–og* in American English (*dialog, catalog*, etc.).
- Words that end in *–ence* in British English end with *–ense* in American English (*pretense, defense, offense*, etc.).
- Words that end with *–amme* in British English usually just end with *–am* in American English (*kilogram, program, telegram*, etc.)
- Words with a double L in the middle in British English (such as *traveller* or *travelling*) usually use a single L in American English (*traveler, traveling*, etc), but some words that use a single L followed by a consonant in British English use a double L in American English (skillful, installment).

There are other spelling differences which do not follow any particular 'rules', and these words have to be learnt individually (for example, *judgement / judgment*).

** This is one of several words that are used in both British and American English, but which have a different meaning (often depending on the context in which they are used). In this case, *faculty* is usually used by North Americans to talk about the people who work in a school, college, university, etc, while in British English it is used to talk about a particular department in a university (e.g., *the Humanities Faculty*). Gas (see 16 across) in American English is a short form of *gasoline*. The word *gasoline* is also used in British English, but the word *petrol* is more common: British-English speakers normally use the word *gas* to talk about a substance that is used to heat the house or cook food. To make things more complicated, it also has the same meaning in North America.

Changes (pages 8 – 9)

Exercise 1.
1. True   **2.** True   **3.** False: there has been an *improvement*   **4.** False: there has been an *increase*   **5.** False: there has been a *strengthening* of the dollar   **6.** False: there has been a *relaxation* of border controls   **7.** False: we're *increasing* or *building up* our stock of coal   **8.** True   **9.** False: there has been a *slight* fall   **10.** False: they're going to *decrease* the number   **11.** False: there has been a *decline*   **12.** False: there has been a *tightening up* of the rules   **13.** False: there has been a *widening* of the gap   **14.** True   **15.** False: there has been a *downward* trend   **16.** True   **17.** True   **18.** True   **19.** True   **20.** False: Americans want to *broaden* their horizons.

Increase, decrease, rise, fall, progress and *cut* are used as nouns in these sentences. These words can also be verbs without changing their form.

Deterioration, weakening, tightening up, growth, relaxation, narrowing, improvement and *expansion* are nouns or noun phrases in these sentences. They can also be used as verbs with a change in their form (*deteriorate, weaken, tighten up, grow, relax, narrow, improve, expand*)

Exercise 2
The words in the box are:
adapt replace expand promote reduce transform switch renovate exchange demote alter disappear vary raise lower extend enlarge heighten lengthen deepen shorten stretch revise amend cut outsource deteriorate streamline upgrade restructure downsize

1. exchanged   **2.** adapt   **3.** transformed   **4.** renovated   5. switched   **6.** vary   **7.** expands   **8.** deteriorating   **9.** revised *or* amended (*revised* prices are usually increased, but they can also go down, as in this example. This verb in this context is usually used in the passive voice)   **10.** stretched

Comparing and contrasting (page 10)

1. contrast   **2.** differ   **3.** differentiate   **4.** characteristics   **5.** distinction   **6.** Compared   **7.** comparison   **8.** similar to   **9.** similarities   **10.** In the same way   **11.** Likewise   **12.** By way of contrast   **13.** Nevertheless / Even so / However (*Even so* is more common in spoken than in written English)   **14.** discrepancy   **15.** whereas

Condition and requirement (page 11)

1. As long as   **2.** Unless   **3.** on condition that (*that* = optional)   **4.** providing that (*that* = optional. We can also say *provided that*)   **5.** preconditions   **6.** In case of (note that in this particular expression, we do not say *In case of a fire*. In other situations, an article or pronoun would be needed after *in case of*)   **7.** in the event of   **8.** stipulation   **9.** unconditional   **10.** Assuming that (*that* = optional)   **11.** on the assumption that   **12.** prerequisites   **13.** terms / conditions   **14.** requirement   **15.** Failing that (*Failing that* means that if the first option – *telephoning us* – is not possible, you should try the second option – *send us an email*)   **16.** otherwise

Confusing words (pages 12 –14)

1. action / activity   **2.** advise / advice   **3.** effect / affect   **4.** alternative / alternate   **5.** appreciable / appreciative   **6.** assumption / presumption   **7.** prevent / avoid   **8.** beside / besides   **9.** shortly / briefly   **10.** canal / channel   **11.** complementary / complimentary   **12.** conscious / conscientious   **13.** continual / continuous   **14.** control / inspect   **15.** objection / criticism   **16.** injury / harm / damage   **17.** disinterested / uninterested *or* disinterested (it is a common misconception in English that *disinterested* cannot be used in the same way as *uninterested* when we want to say that someone does not find something interesting)   **18.** for / while / during   **19.** However / Moreover   **20.** infer / imply   **21.** wounded / injured   **22.** job / work   **23.** lie / lay   **24.** watch / look at   **25.** percent / percentage   **26.** permit / permission   **27.** possibility / chance   **28.** priceless / worthless   **29.** principle / principal / principal / principle   **30.** trouble / problem   **31.** rise / raise   **32.** remember / remind   **33.** objective / subjective   **34.** tolerant / tolerable   **35.** treat / cure

Idioms and colloquialisms 1 (pages 15 – 16)

Here are the most suitable answers:

Exercise 1
1. I really don't mind. It's up to you.   **2.** You've got to be kidding!   **3.** I couldn't agree more.   **4.** Can I take a rain check on that?   **5.** Let me sleep on it.   **6.** It does nothing for me.   **7.** You really should get a life *or* You've got to be kidding!   **8.** I couldn't care less.   **9.** Wow! Way to go!   **10.** Why not? Go for it!   **11.** You're welcome, but it was nothing really.   **12.** Never mind. It can't be helped.

Answer key

Exercise 2

1. Sure. Why not?   **2.** How's it going?   **3.** How should I know?   **4.** What a drag!   **5.** You bet!   **6.** I'm going to give it all I've got.   **7.** Oh, I'm used to it.   **8.** What do you have in mind?   **9.** I'm afraid you're out of luck.   **10.** Let me lend a hand.   **11.** Sorry, I'm a bit tied up right now.   **12.** Is it any wonder?

Idioms and colloquialisms 2 (pages 17 – 18)

Exercise 1

1. I'd be glad to (this is a polite way of agreeing to do something)   **2.** Be my guest (this is a polite way of giving somebody permission to do something)   **3.** A little bird told me (we say this when we don't want to say who said something to us)   **4.** My lips are sealed (we say this when we promise to keep a secret, or when we refuse to tell someone a secret)   **5.** I'm keeping my fingers crossed (we say this when we are hoping that something will happen)   **6.** Rather you than me (this means that we are glad we are not doing something that somebody else is)   **7.** Fire away, I'm all ears (this means that we are ready and eager to listen to something)   **8.** Now you're talking (we say this when somebody suggests something that is more acceptable or enjoyable than something else they have already suggested)   **9.** I'm having second thoughts (this means that we will probably change our mind about something we have already agreed to)   **10.** That'll be the day (this means that we don't believe something will happen. We can also say *And pigs might fly!* or *I'll believe it when I see it*)   **11.** Who let the cat out of the bag? (we say this when we want to know who revealed something that was supposed to be a secret, a surprise, etc)   **12.** That'll teach you! (we say this to someone who has done something bad, and is now suffering the consequences)

Exercise 2

1. This is on me (we say this when we are offering to pay for something)   **2.** Congratulations (this is another way of saying *Well done*)   **3.** I'd love to (we say this when we are accepting an offer to do something)   **4.** You're welcome (this is a polite way of acknowledging someone when they thank you for something. We can also say *Not at all*, *Don't mention it* or *My pleasure*, or sometimes a combination of these, as in this dialog. More informally, we can say *OK* or *No problem*. *No worries* is also sometimes used by younger people)   **5.** Make yourself at home (this is an expression we use when somebody visits our house).   **6.** Hold on (an informal expression which means *Wait*. We can also *say Hang on*)   **7.** Take care and keep in touch (an expression we use when we will not see somebody for a while)   **8.** Couldn't be better (this means that we are very well)   **9.** I'd rather you didn't (this is a polite way of telling somebody that you don't want them to do something)   **10.** That's too bad (this is another way of saying *Hard luck*, *Bad luck* or *Tough luck*, and we use it to sympathize with someone)   **11.** It doesn't ring any bells (this means that you do not recognize the name of someone or something)   **12.** Yes, knock on wood (*Knock on wood* is an expression we use when we hope that something will, or won't, happen)

Exercise 3

1. How's it going? (an informal way of asking somebody if something is going well or badly)   **2.** I'll say (when we agree completely with somebody)   **3.** Not on your life! (an informal way of saying that we would never do something)   **4.** That's a load off my mind (when we are suddenly no longer worried about something that was troubling us. We can also say *That's a weight off my mind*)   **5.** Well, keep it to yourself (= don't tell anyone else, usually because something is, or should be, a secret)   **6.** Sure thing (an informal way of saying we agree to do something)   **7.** Take a seat (*Take a seat* means *Please sit down*)   **8.** Don't kill yourself (this is an informal way of telling somebody not to work too hard, or to calm down, relax)   **9.** It's not the end of the world (this means that things are not as bad as they seem to someone)   **10.** Have a good time (we want the person to whom we are speaking to enjoy themselves)   **11.** So I guess you're in the doghouse again (if you are *in the doghouse*, you are in trouble with someone)   **12.** Gesundheit! (we say this German word, which means *health*, when someone sneezes. We can also say *Bless you!*)

Idioms and colloquialisms 3 (pages 19 – 20)

Exercise 1

1. E   **2.** J   **3.** D   **4.** A   **5.** L   **6.** C   **7.** I   **8.** G   **9.** B   **10.** K   **11.** F   **12.** H

Exercise 2

1. L   **2.** C   **3.** K   **4.** I   **5.** E   **6.** J   **7.** A   **8.** D   **9.** F   **10.** G   **11.** H   **12.** B

Idioms and colloquialisms 4 (pages 21 – 22)

Exercise 1

1. candle   **2.** worms   **3.** bull   **4.** nose   **5.** blind   **6.** track   **7.** pressed   **8.** weather   **9.** blue   **10.** question   **11.** record   **12.** ground   **13.** ice   **14.** air   **15.** shop   **16.** ground   **17.** close   **18.** picture

Exercise 2

1. name   **2.** world   **3.** strings   **4.** played   **5.** red   **6.** good   **7.** out   **8.** ground   **9.** level   **10.** can   **11.** flow   **12.** parade   **13.** leaf   **14.** break   **15.** running   **16.** large   **17.** five   **18.** sixth

Metaphors (pages 23 – 25)

Exercise 1
1. edifice 2. sow the seeds 3. constructed 4. buttressed 5. deep-rooted 6. architect 7. laid the foundations 8. towering or ground-breaking 9. blueprint 10. built up 11. built on 12. under construction 13. collapsed 14. ground-breaking 15. ruins 16. demolished 17. fertile 18. took root 19. stemmed from 20. fruitful

Exercise 2
1. argument 2. intelligence* 3. help 4. important / unimportant 5. effort 6. knowledge 7. opportunity 8. discover or find out 9. life or a career path 10. force 11. discussion 12. problem 13. enthusiasm / excitement 14. successful / failure

* Metaphorically, *intelligence* can also be like a knife or something sharp (e.g., 'He was very *sharp-witted*', 'She was an *incisive* critic')

Modified words (pages 26 – 27)

Exercise 1
1. teleconferences 2. biannual 3. autobiography 4. transformed 5. predetermined 6. semi-final (this can also be written as one word, *semifinal*, or two words, *semi final*) 7. postgraduate 8. co-workers 9. micro-organisms (this can also be written as one word, *microorganisms*, or two words, *micro organisms*) 10. Unisex 11. substandard 12. circumnavigate 13. International 14. monolingual 15. underachiever 16. overpopulated

Exercise 2
1. Microwaves 2. telecommunications 3. unilateral 4. semicircle 5. autopilot 6. bilingual 7. circumvented 8. post-war (this can also be written as one word, *postwar*) 9. premature 10. overweight 11. subconscious 12. coeducational (this can also be written as *co-educational*) 13. underestimated 14. transatlantic (note that *Atlantic* does not begin with a capital letter in this word, but would need to when used on its own) 15. interrelationship 16. monotone

Exercise 3
1. underestimate 2. autobiography 3. Premature 4. Overpopulation 5. co-workers 6. transatlantic 7. Transforming 8. unisex 9. subconsciously 10. biannual

Numbers and symbols (page 28)

1. 2011 = two thousand (and) eleven (some people also say *twenty eleven*) / 1998 = nineteen ninety eight 2. 24/7 = twenty four seven (= 24 hours a day, 7 days a week) 3. 0.8% = zero point eight per cent (we can also say *point eight of a percent*) 4. 3.45 = three forty five, or quarter of four* 5. 1800 = eighteen hundred (hours) 6. 30 June = the thirtieth of June *or* June thirtieth 7. 10/3 = the third of October / October third (in the United States) or the tenth of March / March the tenth (in the United Kingdom). Alternatively, you could say *the third of the tenth* 8. 27½ = twenty seven and a half 9. ¾ = three quarters *or* three fourths 10. 2m x 1m x 1m = two metres by one metre by one metre 11. $1.99 = one dollar ninety nine (or *one dollar and ninety nine cents*) 12. $100.99 = one hundred dollars ninety nine (or *one hundred dollars and ninety nine cents*) 13. $120.75 = one hundred and twenty dollars seventy five (or *one hundred and twenty dollars and seventy five cents*) / $1,120.75 = one thousand, one hundred and twenty dollars seventy five (or *one thousand, one hundred and twenty dollars and seventy five cents*) 14. ACB81 - 25/B = ACB eighty one dash (or *hyphen*) 25 slash (or *stroke*) B 15. 020 7921 3567 = oh two oh, seven nine two one, three five six seven 16. 0845 601 5884 = oh eight four five, six oh one, five double eight four 17. 0800 231415 = oh eight hundred, two three one four one five (or oh eight hundred, twenty three, fourteen, fifteen) 18. 999 = nine nine nine / 911 = nine one one / 000 = triple oh 19. # = hash / 0 = zero / * = star 20. $200K = two hundred thousand dollars / mid-50s = mid-fifties 21. $6M = six million dollars 22. 2:1 = two to one (when talking about odds and ratios) 23. @snailmail.com = at snailmail dot co dot u k 24. GR8 = great / :-) = happy / CUL8R = see you later (informal abbreviations and emoticons** such as these are commonly used in text messages, notes and e-mail) 25. 4x4 = four by four (a vehicle with four-wheel drive, also called a *4WD* or *SUV – Sports Utility Vehicle*) 26. 2:0 = two nil / 3:3 = three all 27. 37,762,418 = thirty seven million, seven hundred and sixty two thousand, four hundred and eighteen 28. 1099 = ten ninety nine (this is a document that people in the United states send to the IRS – the US tax department – that gives details of the money they have earned during the year other than their salary) 29. © = copyright (the material cannot be copied without permission) 30. ® = registered (the name is registered, and cannot be used by another company for another product)

* In British English, people say *(a) quarter to four*. Note that for times before the half hour, people say *past* in British English and *after* in American English (for example, 4.10 is ten *past* four in British English, and ten *after* four in American English).

** :-) is an *emoticon*, a symbol that shows emotion. Emoticons take the form of a face on its side, and use standard punctuation symbols and letters. In this case, it is a smiling face to show happiness. Other emoticons include :-(to show unhappiness, :-0 to show surprise, :-‖ to show anger, :-@ to show fear, :-X to indicate a kiss. Some computers automatically turn some emoticons into proper faces (for example, by entering :-) , the computer automatically makes a ☺).

Answer key

Obligation and option (page 29)

1. required / needed (not *mandatory* or *compulsory*, as these cannot be followed with *by*)   **2.** compulsory (We can also say *obligatory*). **3.** must (not *have*, as this must be followed with *to*)   **4.** have / need   **5.** liable (not *obliged* or *compelled*, as these must be followed with *to*)   **6.** forced (this is better than *obliged* or *compelled*, as it is stronger and suggests that the company has no other choice. Also, *obliged* and *compelled* are usually used when somebody makes somebody else do something)   **7.** exempt **8.** Mandatory (this is better than *Compulsory*, as it suggests the checks must be carried out because of a law)   **9.** voluntary (not *optional*, as the gap is preceded by *a*, not *an*)   **10.** optional / voluntary   **11.** alternative (used as part of an expression: '*We have no alternative but to…*')   **12.** obliged / required   **13.** obligation (note the adjective form of obliged / obligation = *obligatory*) **14.** compelled (in other words, he felt that people were putting pressure on him to make him leave. We could also use *obliged*) **15.** need (used here as a noun)   **16.** essential (*vital* or *imperative* could also be used)

Opinion, attitude and belief (pages 30 – 32)

Exercise 1
1. tolerance   **2.** obsessed   **3.** reckon (this is quite an informal word in this context)   **4.** suspect   **5.** bigoted   **6.** doubt **7.** fanatical   **8.** dedicated   **9.** opinion   **10.** pragmatic   **11.** committed   **12.** regarding   **13.** disapproval   **14.** maintain **15.** concerned   **16.** cynical   **17.** exception   **18.** convinced   **19.** traditional   **20.** conservative

Exercise 2
1. suspicious   **2.** pragmatic   **3.** fanatical   **4.** disapprove   **5.** opinion   **6.** dedication / commitment   **7.** tolerate   **8.** conservative / traditional   **9.** doubt   **10.** maintain / reckon / suspect / doubt

Exercise 3
1. intellectual (this can also be an adjective: *He's very intellectual*)   **2.** stoical (someone who is stoical is *a stoic*)   **3.** tolerant or open-minded   **4.** Republican (a *republican* outside the United States – note the lower-case *r* – is someone who believes in a *republican* political system, i.e., a country that is governed by elected representatives and led by a president)   **5.** Democrat (a *democrat* outside the United States – note the lower-case *d* – is someone who believes in a *democratic* political system, i.e., a country with a system of government in which everyone can vote to elect its leaders)   **6.** open-minded   **7.** anarchist (*anarchy* is a situation where a country has no government. The adjective is *anarchic*)   **8.** pacifist (*pacifism* is the name of the belief) **9.** vegetarian (this can also be an adjective: *vegetarian food*)   **10.** vegan (this can also be an adjective: *a vegan diet*) **11.** superstitious (the noun is *superstition*)   **12.** atheist (*atheism* is the belief that there is no God)   **13.** agnostic (this can also be a noun)   **14.** moderate (this can also be an adjective: *moderate views*)   **15.** opinionated

Opposites 1: Verbs (pages 33 – 35)

Exercise 1
1. rejected   **2.** denied   **3.** retreating   **4.** refused   **5.** attacked   **6.** demolished   **7.** simplified   **8.** abandon   **9.** withdrew **10.** deteriorated   **11.** ignored   **12.** rewarding   **13.** lowered   **14.** set   **15.** fell   **16.** loosen   **17.** succeeded   **18.** postponed **19.** lend   **20.** concealed   **21.** extended   **22.** exaggerate   **23.** replenished   **24.** gained   **25.** abolished   **26.** hired

Exercise 2
Across: **2.** misquoted   **3.** misdiagnosing   **6.** discontinuing   **8.** misrepresent   **10.** unloaded   **12.** disagree   **13.** misuses **14.** unlock   **16.** unfolded   **20.** distrust or mistrust   **22.** disapproves   **23.** disobey
Down: **1.** misjudged   **2.** misunderstands   **4.** disconnecting   **5.** disqualified   **7.** displeased   **9.** miscalculated   **11.** misbehave **15.** disallowed   **17.** misplaced   **18.** uncovered (not *discovered*)   **19.** disproved   **21.** dislike

Opposites 2: Adjectives (pages 36 – 37)

Exercise 1
1. clear   **2.** easy   **3.** graceful   **4.** detrimental   **5.** approximate   **6.** innocent   **7.** even   **8.** scarce   **9.** flexible **10.** considerable   **11.** crude   **12.** delicate   **13.** dim   **14.** compulsory   **15.** reluctant   **16.** archaic   **17.** worthwhile **18.** vibrant   **19.** tedious   **20.** spontaneous   **21.** intricate   **22.** worthless   **23.** negligible   **24.** feasible   **25.** commonplace **26.** problematic   **27.** smooth   **28.** artificial

Exercise 2
Task 1.
unacceptable inaccurate inadequate disadvantaged disagreeable unattractive unauthorized unavoidable unbelievable uncertain uncomfortable incompetent incomplete unconscious discontented unconvincing incorrect incurable uneven unfair unfashionable dishonest disinclined illegal unlimited illiterate illogical unmarried immature immoral immortal disobedient disorganized impatient imperfect impersonal impossible improper impure unqualified (*disqualified* is a verb which means to make someone not able to do something: '*He was disqualified from driving for a year*')   irrational irregular irrelevant irreplaceable irresistible irresolute irresponsible unsatisfactory dissatisfied insufficient unwelcome

Note that adjectives which end with *–ful* are usually made into their opposite form by changing *–ful* to *–less* (*thoughtful* = *thoughtless*, *useful* = *useless*, etc.). *Helpful* is one exception to this rule (the opposite is *unhelpful*. *Help<u>less</u>* has a different meaning, and means *not able to do anything*)

<u>Task 2.</u>
1. uninclined = disinclined   **2.** inhonest = dishonest   **3.** imsufficient = insufficient   **4.** unresponsible = irresponsible
5. inconvincing = unconvincing   **6.** disadequate = inadequate

Phrasal verbs 1 (pages 38 – 39)

<u>Exercise 1</u>
1. bring up   **2.** face up to   **3.** call off   **4.** count on   **5.** catch up with   **6.** die down   **7.** drop out of   **8.** figure out   **9.** fell out
10. find   **11.** grow up   **12.** keep up with   **13.** leaves out   **14.** pointed out   **15.** look into   **16.** brought up   **17.** fall behind
18. cut down on

<u>Exercise 2</u>
1. taken over   **2.** put forward   **3.** pull through   **4.** done away with   **5.** look into   **6.** carry out   **7.** went, kept *or* carried on
8. wear off   **9.** turn up   **10.** picked up   **11.** put across   **12.** ran into   **13.** set...back   **14.** look back on   **15.** turned out
16. turned away   **17.** works out to   **18.** cut off

Phrasal verbs 2 (pages 40 – 41)
<u>Exercise 1</u>
1. get   **2.** look *or* go   **3.** get   **4.** get   **5.** look   **6.** go   **7.** get   **8.** went   **9.** look   **10.** look   **11.** came   **12.** look   **13.** get
14. give   **15.** came   **16.** go   **17.** getting   **18.** go

<u>Exercise 2</u>
1. came   **2.** give   **3.** go *or* look   **4.** get   **5.** came   **6.** get   **7.** give   **8.** go   **9.** come *or* go   **10.** came   **11.** come   **12.** getting
13. comes   **14.** get   **15.** give   **16.** look   **17.** give   **18.** got *or* came

Phrasal verbs 3 (pages 42 – 44)

<u>Across:</u>
1. put down   **5.** talk ... round   **6.** take after   **7.** running up against   **9.** turn...out   **10.** picked on   **11.** opt out   **16.** turned up
19. set off   **20.** run up   **22.** set aside (or *put aside*)   **24.** take to   **28.** take up   **30.** held up   **32.** engaged in   **36.** set off
37. factoring in   **38.** running out   **39.** handing in

<u>Down:</u>
1. put aside (*set aside* – see *22 across* – has the same meaning, but would not work in the crossword grid)   **2.** take in
3. add up to   **4.** taken in   **6.** turned down   **8.** put up with   **12.** taken apart   **13.** set...against   **14.** make out   **15.** made...up
17. ran for   **18.** pick up   **21.** make up for   **23.** set up   **25.** kick in   **26.** stemmed from   **27.** pull out   **29.** shut out of
31. bring about   **33.** gone down with   **34.** break into   **35.** went for

Presenting an argument (page 45)

1. However   **2.** First of all / Firstly   **3.** As well as / In addition to   **4.** I believe / I think   **5.** Moreover / Furthermore   **6.** Although
/ While   **7.** as well   **8.** Nevertheless   **9.** The most important reason / The main reason   **10.** As far as I am concerned / For me
11. Many consider   **12.** Secondly   **13.** Finally   **14.** In other words   **15.** In conclusion / To summarize   **16.** On the one hand
17. On the other hand   **18.** In my opinion

When you are asked to present an argument, you should always look at it from two sides, giving reasons why you agree and / or disagree before reaching a conclusion. It is usually best to present your strongest argument in favor of something just before the conclusion.

Pronouns and determiners (pages 46 – 47)

<u>Exercise 1</u>
1. there   **2.** their   **3.** it   **4.** them (used when we do not specify if the caller was male or female)   **5.** himself   **6.** they   **7.** that
8. which   **9.** yours   **10.** yourself   **11.** its (do not confuse the possessive *its* with *it's*, which is a contraction of *it is* or *it has*)
12. There   **13.** that   **14.** them   **15.** which   **16.** itself   **17.** it   **18.** they   **19.** those   **20.** itself   **21.** herself   **22.** that or which
(alternatively, you could leave the space blank. *That* or *which*, when used as pronouns in defining relative clauses such as this, can
be left out when they are the object of the relative clause)   **23.** whose   **24.** ourselves   **25.** theirs

Answer key

<u>Exercise 2</u>
1. **that**   2. **which**   3. th**ere**   4. the**m**   5. tho**se**   6. th**ey**   7. its**el**f   8. oursel**ve**s   9. th**ei**r   10. it**s**

The 'hidden' word is *themselves* (e.g., *As it became obvious an economic crisis was looming, the Republicans were divided among* <u>*themselves*</u> *as to the best course of action to take.*)

Similar meanings: Adjectives 1 (pages 48 – 49)

1. abrupt   **2.** robust   **3.** rudimentary   **4.** nominal   **5.** conventional   **6.** curious   **7.** expert   **8.** remote   **9.** absurd
10. compatible   **11.** legitimate   **12.** rigid   **13.** placid   **14.** narrow   **15.** covert   **16.** negligible   **17.** hazardous
18. contemporary   **19.** enduring   **20.** exceptional   **21.** outlandish   **22.** prompt   **23.** outdated   **24.** prospective
25. comprehensive   **26.** adequate   **27.** gradual   **28.** dramatic   **29.** thriving   **30.** complex   **31.** inventive   **32.** potent
33. radical   **34.** shallow   **35.** erratic   **36.** fertile   **37.** even   **38.** crucial / indispensable   **39.** varied.   **40.** crucial / indispensable
41. toxic   **42.** incisive   **43.** finite   **44.** widespread   **45.** resolute   **46.** coarse

Similar meanings: Adjectives 2 (page 50)

1. concise   **2.** handsome   **3.** archaic   **4.** risky   **5.** abundant   **6.** chaotic   **7.** tedious   **8.** evident   **9.** rampant   **10.** integral
11. scrupulous   **12.** tenacious   **13.** industrious   **14.** credible

The word in the shaded vertical strip is *characteristic*.

Similar meanings: Nouns (pages 51 – 53)

<u>Exercise 1</u>
1. agenda / schedule   **2.** accommodations / housing   **3.** discipline / order   **4.** assistance / help   **5.** drop / decline
6. faults / defects   **7.** opposition / resistance   **8.** proof / evidence   **9.** discount / reduction   **10.** proximity / closeness
11. appointment / meeting   **12.** acclaim / praise   **13.** work / employment   **14.** benefits / advantages   **15.** requirements /
prerequisites   **16.** means / method

<u>Exercise 2</u>
1. protest / demonstration   **2.** code / rules   **3.** liability / responsibility   **4.** choices / options   **5.** overview / (short) description
6. magnitude / importance   **7.** cooperation / collaboration   **8.** valid / good   **9.** zenith / peak   **10.** questions / queries
11. characteristics / features (with illnesses, we can also say *symptoms*)   **12.** problems / complications   **13.** strategy / plan
14. priority / precedence   **15.** alterations / changes   **16.** winner / victor

<u>Exercise 3</u>
1. reviews / write-ups   **2.** advent / appearance   **3.** charisma / (personal) appeal   **4.** category / classification   **5.** ending /
termination   **6.** inventions (or achievements) / innovations   **7.** numbers / concentrations   **8.** specialist / expert   **9.** backing /
support   **10.** notion / idea   **11.** parts / components   **12.** achievement / accomplishment   **13.** ultimatum / final demand
14. disparity / difference   **15.** proceeds / earnings   **16.** argument / dispute

Note that many of the words in this exercise might have another meaning if used in a different context. Use a dictionary to check which ones.

Some other nouns with similar meanings to each other include:

admission + access, amenities + facilities, appeal + petition, component + element, discussion + deliberation, exhibit + display, fallacy + misconception, implication + suggestion, poll + survey, results + consequences, victory + triumph

When you keep a written record of words that you learn, you might find it useful to put them into related groups. This would include putting words with the same or a similar meaning together. Remember that you should also record words in context (in other words, you should show how they work in a sentence with other words).

Similar meanings: Verbs 1 (pages 54 – 56)

<u>Across</u>
2. direct   **4.** assume   **5.** attain   **6.** detect   **11.** reveal   **12.** assert   **13.** resist   **14.** refine   **15.** evolve   **16.** convey   **19.** settle
21. relate   **23.** submit   **25.** change   **27.** baffle   **29.** answer   **32.** verify   **33.** enrich   **35.** remove   **36.** exceed   **37.** derive

Answer key

1. accuse   **3.** handle   **7.** create   **8.** elicit   **9.** forbid   **10.** hasten   **12.** affect   **14.** refuse   **17.** gather   **18.** oblige (usually used in the passive form: '*Under the college rules, students are obliged to refrain…*')   **20.** endure   **22.** obtain   **24.** misuse   **26.** assist   **28.** launch   **30.** mirror   **31.** demand   **34.** permit

Note that some of the words above could have a different meaning in another context. For example, in number 8 down, *elicit* has a similar meaning to *obtain*. In another context, it could mean '*to make someone react in a particular way*' (for example, '*His comments elicited a positive response from everyone in the room*'). This is one reason why you should always record the new words that you meet in context, and with an example that shows how they are used. That way, when you use these words yourself, you use them correctly. A good dictionary with sample sentences is extremely useful in this respect.

Also note that although a word might have a similar meaning to another word, it is not always possible to use that word as a direct substitute in a sentence.

Similar meanings: Verbs 2 (pages 57 – 59)

Exercise 1
1. crush   **2.** heighten   **3.** attract   **4.** replacing   **5.** exemplifies   **6.** supported   **7.** recover   **8.** explain   **9.** exhaust   **10.** achieve   **11.** prevented   **12.** portray   **13.** measure   **14.** encourage   **15.** highlight   **16.** hastened

Exercise 2
1. proved   **2.** solve   **3.** increase   **4.** include   **5.** dictated   **6.** forfeit   **7.** created   **8.** control   **9.** encouraging   **10.** produce   **11.** suspect   **12.** protect   **13.** constrained   **14.** accepted   **15.** check   **16.** exhibit

Exercise 3
1. realized   **2.** prospered   **3.** surpassed   **4.** understood   **5.** improved   **6.** address   **7.** relating   **8.** originated   **9.** manage   **10.** examined   **11.** remove   **12.** supposed   **13.** produce   **14.** achieve   **15.** settled   **16.** build

Note that while all of these words have a similar meaning to the underlined words in the sentences, not all of them could be used to *replace* those words without partly changing the meaning of the sentence.

Spelling (page 60)

Exercise 1

The incorrectly-spelt words are underlined and corrected below.

1

Despite banning tobacco advertising and raising the price of cigarettes, the government's anti-smoking campaign has failed to have any long-term effects. It is now widely believed that more drastic measures are necessary. A new national committee, which has been formed to tackle the problem, has made several recommendations. These include banning smoking in all public areas, and denying hospital treatment to persistent smokers who have been warned by their doctors to give up but failed to do so.

2

It is arguable whether good pronunciation is more important than good grammar and vocabulary. Conscientious students balance their acquisition of these skills, hoping to achieve both fluency and accuracy. English teachers should encourage their students to practice all the relevant language skills, and use their English at every opportunity.

3

It is becoming increasingly difficult for many people to find decent accommodation in the city at a price they can afford. To put it simply, there are too many people and not enough homes for them. Local community centers and charitable organizations such as *Home Front* can offer advice, but it is widely agreed that the situation is no longer manageable. The fact that some councils in the city are building cheap, temporary housing for lower-paid professionals is the only official acknowledgment of this problem.

Exercise 2
1. reversible   **2.** professional   **3.** criticize   **4.** necessary   **5.** beginning   **6.** perceive   **7.** indispensable   **8.** referring   **9.** liaison   **10.** tendency   **11.** definitely   **12.** embarrass   **13.** ✓   **14.** ✓   **15.** responsible   **16.** separate   **17.** questionnaire   **18.** minuscule   **19.** integrate   **20.** ✓   **21.** weird   **22.** irresistible   **23.** achievement   **24.** millennium   **25.** occurrence   **26.** independent   **27.** supersede   **28.** harassment

Answer key

Starting and stopping (pages 61 – 62)

Exercise 1
The words and phrases in the box are:
abolish   arise   back out   cancel   cease   closure   delete   deter   discontinue   dismiss   dissuade   embark   eradicate   establish   expel   fire   freeze   inception   initiate   kick off   launch   outbreak   phase in   phase out   prevent   pull out   quash   quit   resign   retire   set off   set up   suppress   suspend   take off   take up   turn down

Exercise 2
1. canceled   **2.** deleted   **3.** backed out *or* pulled out   **4.** outbreak   **5.** set up *or* established   **6.** embarking *or* setting off   **7.** suppress *or* quash   **8.** eradicated   **9.** deter *or* prevent *or* dissuade   **10.** dissuade / initiated   **11.** launched / took off   **12.** suspended   **13.** took up   **14.** phased in / phased out   **15.** inception / closure   **16.** ceased   **17.** retiring   **18.** quit (= informal) *or* resign / fired (= informal) or dismissed   **19.** turn…down   **20.** freeze   **21.** discontinued   **22.** abolish   **23.** kick off (= informal)   **24.** arisen   **25.** expelled *or* suspended

Task commands (page 63)

Exercise 1
1. F   **2.** D   **3.** C   **4.** H   **5.** A   **6.** G   **7.** B   **8.** E

Exercise 2
1. D   **2.** G   **3.** A   **4.** H   **5.** E   **6.** B   **7.** C   **8.** F

Other words and phrases which you might find useful include:
calculate, characterize, classify, comment on, consider, deduce, describe, determine, differentiate between, distinguish between, evaluate, explain, give an account of, identify, list, show, state, summarize

Time (pages 64 – 65)

Exercise 1

Part 1:
1. Prior to (this phrase is usually followed by a noun or by an –ing verb. For example: *Prior to moving to the country, he had to learn the language*)   **2.** By the time   **3.** Formerly (we could also use *Previously*, but *Formerly* works better in this context)   **4.** precede   **5.** Previously   **6.** Earlier (we could also use *Previously*)

Part 2:
1. While (we can also say *As* or *Just as*. Note that *while* is usually used to talk about long actions. For short actions, we would use *when*)   **2.** During (we can also say *Throughout*. *During* and *throughout* are followed by a noun)   **3.** In the meantime   **4.** At that very moment

Part 3:
1. Following (this word is always followed by a noun. We can also say *after*)   **2.** As soon as (we can also say *Once* or *The moment / minute that*. These words and phrases are always followed by an action: *Once the show had ended, we went home*)   **3.** Afterwards

Exercise 2
(1) In the past: a few decades ago, at that point / moment in history, at the turn of the century, back in the 1990s, between 2003 and 2005, from 2006 to 2011, in medieval times, in my childhood / youth, in those days, last century
(2) The past leading to the present: ever since, for the past few months, lately, over the past six weeks
(3) The present: as things stand, nowadays, these days
(4) The future: by the end of this year, for the foreseeable future, for the next few weeks, from now on, in another five years' time, one day, over the coming weeks and months, sooner or later

Exercise 3
1. = (q): to make some of your time available for a particular purpose.   **2.** = (o): to like someone or something a lot.   **3.** = (a): someone or something that is in a time warp seems old-fashioned because they have not changed when other people and things have changed.   **4.** = (s) or (f): to make some of your time available for a particular purpose. This expression is often used in the negative.   **5.** = (n): earlier than necessary.   **6.** = (t): a spoken expression used for saying that someone should do something now, instead of waiting to do it later.   **7.** = (e): an expression that is usually spoken, which means that you are annoyed because something has happened later than it should.   **8.** = (b): usually.   **9.** = (r): used for telling someone to hurry.   **10.** = (d): used for talking about what will happen at some future time.   **11.** = (i): a spoken expression used for saying that you will know in the future whether something is true or right.   **12.** = (p): to make time seem to pass more quickly by doing something instead of just waiting.   **13.** = (j): to change and become modern.   **14.** = (c): used for saying that something is strange or surprising.   **15.** = (l): the second time that something happens. Also *the first time around*, *the third time around*, etc.   **16.** = (m): much more modern or advanced than other people or things.   **17.** = (h): sometimes, but not often.   **18.** = (g): for the present.   **19.** = (k): for a long period of time.   **20.** = (f): used for talking about things that happen fairly often.

Answer key

Word association: Adjectives (pages 66 – 67)

1. important **2.** material **3.** objective **4.** major **5.** central **6.** rational **7.** damaging **8.** rapid **9.** false **10.** careful
11. popular **12.** critical **13.** particular **14.** essential **15.** modest **16.** impossible **17.** interested **18.** positive **19.** noticeable
20. lengthy **21.** severe **22.** realistic

Word association: Nouns (Pages 68 – 70)

Across
1. background **5.** effect **7.** accent **8.** guess **11.** advice **12.** consideration **14.** suggestion **15.** instruction **17.** solution
19. permission **20.** difficulty **21.** qualification **22.** opportunity **25.** estimate **29.** appeal **32.** evidence **33.** medicine **34.** reason

Down
2. accident **3.** responsibility **4.** agreement **6.** features **9.** behavior **10.** career **12.** contribution **13.** description
16. criticism **18.** investigation **23.** respect **24.** method **26.** sequence **27.** judgment **28.** project **30.** progress **31.** lesson

Word association: Verbs (pages 71 – 73)

Exercise 1
1. influence **2.** obtain **3.** discuss **4.** settle **5.** encourage **6.** comply **7.** devise **8.** uncover **9.** deserve
The word in the shaded vertical strip is *undermine*.

Exercise 2
1. inspire **2.** object **3.** argue **4.** oppose **5.** fight **6.** highlight **7.** change **8.** undertake **9.** differ
The word in the shaded vertical strip is *negotiate*.

Exercise 3
1. approve **2.** listen **3.** dismiss **4.** abandon **5.** fall **6.** combat **7.** underline **8.** conclude **9.** overcome
The word in the shaded vertical strip is *reinforce*.

Word forms: Nouns from verbs (pages 74 – 75)

Exercise 1

Remove 2 letters, then add 4 letters:	provide = provision persuade = persuasion recognize = recognition abolish = abolition decide = decision
Remove 1 letter, then add 7 letters:	qualify = qualification apply = application identify = identification notify = notification imply = implication
Remove 1 letter, then add 5 letters:	consume = consumption admire = admiration permit = permission determine = determination compete = competition
Remove 1 letter, then add 4 letters:	argue = argument assure = assurance intervene = intervention expand = expansion produce = production
Remove 1 letter, then add 3 letters:	negotiate = negotiation expose = exposure supervise = supervision behave = behavior promote = promotion
Remove 1 letter, then add 2 letters:	refuse = refusal survive = survival arrive = arrival rehearse = rehearsal respond = response
Add 3 letters:	fail = failure coincide = coincidence warn = warning suggest = suggestion prohibit = prohibition
Add 4 letters:	disturb = disturbance attend = attendance require = requirement manage = management prefer = preference
Add 5 letters:	sign = signature expect = expectation recommend = recommendation consult = consultation relax = relaxation

Answer key

Exercise 2
1. acquisition (from *acquire*)   **2.** choice (from *choose*)   **3.** criticism (from *criticize*)   **4.** emphasis (from *emphasize*)   **5.** labor (from *labor*: no change is needed)   **6.** loss (from *lose*)   **7.** maintenance (from *maintain*)   **8.** scrutiny (from *scrutinize*)   **9.** solution (from *solve*)   **10.** subscription (from *subscribe*)

The verb / noun in the shaded strip is *compromise*.

Word forms: Nouns from adjectives (pages 76 – 77)

Exercise 1
1. value   **2.** taste   **3.** thirst   **4.** honesty   **5.** confidence   **6.** expense   **7.** restrictions   **8.** similarities   **9.** certainty **10.** absenteeism (or *absence*)   **11.** convenience   **12.** necessity   **13.** relaxation   **14.** flexibility   **15.** safety   **16.** responsibility **17.** accuracy   **18.** profession   **19.** complications   **20.** difference   **21.** charisma   **22.** addiction   **23.** Constitution (note that this particular example begins with a capital letter)   **24.** investigation   **25.** justification   **26.** reality

Exercise 2
Remove 4 letters: comfortable = comfort   fashionable = fashion   systematic = system
Remove 3 letters, then add 5 letters: long = length   high = height   strong = strength
Remove 3 letters, then add 1 letter: optimistic = optimism   pessimistic = pessimism   realistic = realism (*reality* is also a noun form)
Remove 2 letters, then add 5 letters: able = ability   available = availability   compatible = compatibility
Remove 2 letters, then add 3 letters: hot = heat   deep = depth   confused = confusion
Remove 2 letters, then add 2 letters: aggressive = aggression   creative = creation   appreciative = appreciation
Remove 2 letters: functional = function   logical = logic   optional = option
Remove 1 letter, then add 3 letters: considerate = consideration   mature = maturity   secure = security
Remove 1 letter, then add 2 letters: convenient = convenience   sufficient = sufficiency   true = truth
Add 2 letters: bored = boredom   loyal = loyalty   warm = warmth
Add 3 letters: familiar = familiarity   popular = popularity   punctual = punctuality
Add 4 letters: aware = awareness   serious = seriousness   weak = weakness

Word forms: Adjectives from verbs (page 78)

1. promotional / inspiring   **2.** innovative / impressive   **3.** wasteful / obligatory   **4.** repetitive / boring   **5.** excited / doubtful **6.** decisive / active   **7.** inventive / changeable   **8.** continual (= stopping and starting) / continuous (without stopping) **9.** approachable / frightening   **10.** convincing / critical   **11.** inclusive / competitive   **12.** helpful / supportive / dependable **13.** rectifiable / preferable   **14.** negotiable / refundable   **15.** restricted / valid   **16.** voluntary / constructive   **17.** avoidable / careless (not *careful*)   **18.** creative / imaginative / admirable   **19.** specific / occupational   **20.** attractive / excellent

Working words (pages 79 – 80)

Exercise 1
1. to, no, of   **2.** ago, used, These   **3.** can *or* may, if *or* providing   **4.** Between, over   **5.** most, near   **6.** be, on   **7.** Unless, for *or* on   **8.** at, knowing *or* realizing, would   **9.** spite, managed   **10.** as, anybody *or* anyone   **11.** working, on   **12.** who, just *or* recently   **13.** with, made   **14.** by, had   **15.** the, where   **16.** By, had, this *or* that, off   **17.** missed, too   **18.** What's, quite, also

Exercise 2
1. up, until, two, these *or* those   **2.** which, one, best *or* better, in   **3.** least, more, as *or* since, had   **4.** what, from, else   **5.** going, the other   **6.** been, for, no   **7.** to *or* until, might *or* would (with a change in meaning), they, or   **8.** being, to, a, on   **9.** From, but, a *or* their   **10.** only, on, their, unless, itself   **11.** on, be, a lot *or* much   **12.** borrowing, for, breaking   **13.** any, by, on, held **14.** had to, arrive *or* get, in   **15.** spent, for, eventually *or* finally   **16.** wish, would, for   **17.** in, have been, a *or* one   **18.** for, could, to lend

Children and the family (pages 81 – 82)

Exercise 1
1. Adolescence / adolescent   **2.** minor   **3.** siblings   **4.** separated / divorced   **5.** foster family / foster child / foster   **6.** juvenile **7.** well-adjusted / running wild *or* rebellious   **8.** formative years   **9.** adopt   **10.** teenager   **11.** infant / infancy   **12.** Raise / bring up   **13.** extended family / nuclear family   **14.** strict / authoritarian / lenient   **15.** dependent (note that in British English, the noun is *dependant*)

Exercise 3
1. formative years   **2.** divorced   **3.** brought up   **4.** foster family   **5.** authoritarian   **6.** upbringing   **7.** running wild **8.** adolescence   **9.** juvenile delinquency   **10.** responsible   **11.** siblings   **12.** well-adjusted   **13.** lenient   **14.** over-protective **15.** nuclear   **16.** single-parent family   **17.** dependents   **18.** extended

Answer key

Education (pages 83 – 84)

Exercise 1

1. on line course / night class / day release   **2.** SAT   **3.** lesson / class (in either order)   **4.** lecture / subject or topic / lecturer / seminar / tutorial / tutor   **5.** Literacy / Numeracy   **6.** prospectus / enroll (the British-English spelling is *enrol*)   **7.** faculty   **8.** Physical education   **9.** public school / private school / fees   **10.** kindergarten / grade / elementary school / grade school   **11.** syllabus   **12.** junior high school / middle school (in either order) / high school   **13.** semester / quarter   **14.** graduate / graduate school / higher degree

Exercise 3

1. skills   **2 / 3.** literacy / numeracy (in either order)   **4.** kindergarten / elementary school   **5.** elementary   **6.** secondary   **7.** discipline   **8.** pass   **9.** qualifications   **10.** acquire   **11.** physical education   **12.** graduate   **13.** higher   **14.** degree   **15.** subject   **16.** graduate school   **17.** doctorate   **18.** night class   **19.** day release   **20.** on line course   **21.** mature   **22.** opportunity

Food and diet (pages 85 - 86)

Exercise 1

1. Fiber (spelt *fibre* in British English) / fat / saturated / monosaturated   **2.** Calories / Protein / Calcium / Carbohydrates   **3.** diet / fat farm / exercise   **4.** Organic / Free range / Genetically modified (GM)   **5.** eating disorder / bulimia / anorexia (these last two in either order)   **6.** vegetarian / vegan   **7.** Fast food / junk food / nutritious   **8.** overweight / obese / obesity / diabetes / heart disease   **9.** salmonella / listeria (in either order) / food poisoning   **10.** food groups   **11.** balanced diet   **12.** food intolerance / allergy / allergic

Exercise 2

1. fast food / junk food   **2.** processed   **3.** vitamins / minerals   **4.** minerals / vitamins   **5.** fat / carbohydrates   **6.** carbohydrates / fat   **7.** obesity   **8.** malnourished   **9.** shortages   **10.** harvest   **11.** cholesterol   **12.** balanced diet   **13.** fresh   **14.** fiber

The media (pages 87 – 88)

Exercise 1

1. Slander (this can also be a verb: *to slander* someone) / slanderous / Libel (this can also be a verb: *to libel* someone) / libelous   **2.** read between the lines   **3.** Invasion of privacy   **4.** broadsheet / tabloid / gutter press / Tabloid TV (note that several newspapers that were previously printed on large sheets of paper are now printed on smaller sheets of paper, with the result that *broadsheet* is not used so much any more. It is becoming increasingly common to refer to the old broadsheets as *quality papers*, and tabloids as *popular papers*)   **5.** dumbing down   **6.** journalist / reporter (also known as a *correspondent*)   **7.** censorship (the verb is *to censor*)   **8.** media tycoon (also called a *media baron*)   **9.** Reality TV   **10.** documentary / current affairs   **11.** Check book journalism   **12.** Airtime / Coverage / readership

Exercise 3

1. informed   **2.** broadsheets   **3.** coverage   **4.** current affairs   **5.** journalists or reporters   **6.** reporters or journalists   **7.** tabloids   **8.** broadcasts or programs   **9.** documentaries   **10.** Internet   **11.** Web sites   **12.** download   **13.** information *or* entertainment   **14.** entertainment *or* information   **15.** gutter press   **16.** invasion of privacy   **17.** paparazzi   **18.** libel   **19.** check book journalism   **20.** unscrupulous   **21.** dumbing down   **22.** reality TV   **23.** on line   **24.** censorship *or* restrictions   **25.** freedom of the press

Money and finance (pages 89 – 91)

Exercise 1

1. expenditure   **2.** borrow   **3.** refund   **4.** bankrupt   **5.** balance   **6.** in the black   **7.** receipt   **8.** loss   **9.** exorbitant   **10.** invest   **11.** salary   **12.** priceless   **13.** withdraw   **14.** overcharged   **15.** Frugal *or* Economical   **16.** check   **17.** debited (*debited* is a formal word, and is usually used in the passive: *Your account will be debited on the first day of the month*)   **18.** savings and loan association   **19.** mortgage   **20.** overdraft

Exercise 3

1. borrow   **2.** loan   **3.** income   **4.** expenditure   **5.** overdraft   **6.** cost of living   **7.** Inflation   **8.** economize   **9.** savings and loan association   **10.** interest   **11.** on credit   **12.** exorbitant   **13.** save   **14.** reductions   **15.** bargain   **16.** discount   **17.** invest   **18.** stocks   **19.** shares   **20.** priceless

Nature and the environment (pages 92 – 93)

Exercise 1

1. green belt   **2.** biodegradable packaging   **3.** greenhouse gases   **4.** rainforest   **5.** erosion   **6.** recycle   **7.** organic   **8.** genetically modified (often shortened to *GM*)   **9.** deforestation   **10.** acid rain   **11.** ecosystem   **12.** emissions / fossil fuels   **13.** contaminated (or *polluted*)   **14.** environmentalists   **15.** global warming

Answer key

Exercise 3

1. fossil fuels   **2.** acid rain   **3.** greenhouse gases / CFC gases   **4.** global warming   **5.** rainforest   **6.** contaminated   **7.** emissions / gases   **8.** Poaching   **9.** endangered species   **10.** ecosystem   **11.** recycle   **12.** biodegradable   **13.** genetically modified   **14.** organic   **15.** pollution   **16.** environmentalists   **17.** conservation programs   **18.** battery farming   **19.** green belts

On the road (pages 94 – 95)

Exercise 1

1. Incorrect. *Rush hour* is the time of day when there are a lot of vehicles on the road because most people are traveling to or from work.   **2.** Incorrect. <u>Part</u> of its operating costs are paid for by the government or a local authority.   **3.** Incorrect. In the United States, a *traffic school* is a school where drivers are sent to correct their bad driving (usually offered as an alternative to another form of punishment such as a fine or prison sentence when the driver has done something dangerous or caused an accident).   **4.** Correct.   **5.** Correct.   **6.** Incorrect. *Traffic calming* refers to methods used to slow down traffic in towns and cities (for example, by building raised areas across roads). It is a British-English expression that is becoming more widely used in the United States.   **7.** Incorrect. The *interstate* is a wide road with several lanes of traffic going in each direction, built for fast travel over long distances as part of a national road system.   **8.** Correct.   **9.** Correct.   **10.** Incorrect. *Back out* is another expression for *to reverse* (to move a car backwards).   **11.** Correct.   **12.** Incorrect. A *traffic-free zone* is an area where you cannot drive a vehicle (including, in some cases and at some times, bicycles).   **13.** Incorrect. *Fatalities* are people who are killed in accidents on the road.   **14.** Correct   **15.** Correct   **16.** Incorrect. A *sidewalk* is an area to the side of a road where people can walk.

Exercise 3

1 / 2. injuries / fatalities (in either order)   **3.** speeding   **4.** speed limit   **5.** drink-driving   **6.** pedestrians   **7.** crosswalks   **8.** traffic light   **9 / 10.** congestion / pollution (in either order)   **11.** black spot   **12.** transport strategy   **13.** Traffic-calming   **14.** Park and ride   **15.** traffic-free zone / pedestrian mall   **16.** cycle lanes   **17.** subsidized   **18.** fines   **19.** dominate   **20.** traffic school

Science and technology (pages 96 – 97)

Exercise 1

1. Genetic engineering   **2.** safeguard (this can also be a verb: *to safeguard*)   **3.** Biology (the adjective is *biological*. A scientist who studies living things is a *biologist*)   **4.** technophobe (the fear or distrust of technology is called *technophobia*. A *technophile* is someone who is very enthusiastic about technology)   **5.** breakthrough   **6.** Information technology   **7.** modified   **8.** geneticist   **9.** Cybernetics   **10.** technocrat   **11.** Research (this can also be a verb: *to research*)   **12.** Cryogenics   **13.** experiment (this can also be a verb, *to experiment*. The adjective is *experimental*)   **14.** Life expectancy   **15.** Innovation (the verb is *to innovate*. The adjective is *innovative*)

Exercise 3

1. discovered   **2.** life expectancy   **3.** innovations / inventions   **4.** breakthrough   **5.** invented   **6.** Internet   **7.** e-mail   **8.** research   **9.** technophiles   **10.** technophobes   **11.** cybernetics   **12.** nuclear engineering   **13.** safeguards   **14.** genetic engineering   **15.** analyzed   **16.** experiment   **17.** control

Town and country (pages 98 – 99)

Exercise 1 (the letters in **bold** show you the letters that need to go in the grid)

1. pro**s**pects   **2.** metr**o**polis   **3.** infra**s**tructure   **4.** co**m**muter   **5.** **o**utskirts   **6.** De**p**opulation   **7.** C**o**ngestion   **8.** melting po**t**   **9.** M**i**gration   **10.** st**r**essful   **11.** Urb**a**n (the opposite is *rural*)   **12.** ame**n**ities

The word that fits in the grid is *cosmopolitan*.

Exercise 3

1. metropolis   **2.** cosmopolitan   **3.** urban   **4.** amenities   **5.** cultural events   **6.** infrastructure   **7.** commuters   **8.** Central Business District   **9.** rush hour / peak periods   **10.** congestion   **11.** pollution   **12.** cost of living   **13.** building sites   **14.** population explosion   **15.** drug abuse / street crime   **16.** inner city   **17.** rural   **18.** prospects   **19.** productive land / cultivation / arable land   **20.** urban sprawl   **21.** environment

Travel (pages 100 – 101)

Exercise 1

1. *Persona non grata* is a Latin expression that is used in English. It is most commonly used to refer to someone who is not allowed in a country because they do not have formal permission to be there (for example, their visa for that country has expired, or their passport is no longer valid)   **2.** culture shock   **3.** A *travel agent* is someone whose job is to help people plan holidays and make travel arrangements (they usually work for a *travel agency*). A *tour operator* is a company that organizes holiday tours and then sells them, usually through a travel agency.   **4.** excursion   **5.** coach class (called *economy* or *tourist class* in British English) / First Class

/ Business Class (sometimes also called by other names, including *Club Class*)   **6.** You would probably not be happy. If you are *deported*, you are sent out of the country you are in (maybe because you have done something wrong)   **7.** mass tourism   **8.** A *package tourist* goes on a *package tour*, where they pay for all flights, transfers, accommodation, etc., together and in advance, usually through a travel agency. An *independent traveler* books different aspects of their trip separately (for example, they might book their flight on the Internet, then get a taxi from the airport to their hotel, pay for their hotel when they arrive at their destination, etc.) and does not usually rely on an agency   **9.** No. A *refugee* is someone who leaves their country because they have to (usually because of a war or other threatening event). An *expatriate* is someone who chooses to live and work in another country   **10.** UNHCR = *United Nations High Commission for Refugees*, the department of the United Nations that deals with the problem of *refugees* (see number 9) and other *displaced* people (= people who have been forcibly moved from their home, town, country, etc.: see number 16)   **11.** Ecotourism (also called *green tourism* or sometimes *responsible tourism*)   **12.** Someone who has been *repatriated* has been sent back from one country to the country that is legally their own (possibly because they have been *deported* – see number 6).   **13.** A *cruise* is a journey on a ship for pleasure, especially one that involves visiting a series of places. A *safari* is a journey taken in order to watch or take pictures of wild animals   **14.** If a person is not from the United States, but wants to live and work there, a *green card* is an official document that allows them to do this.   **15.** They are doing something that is illegal: *trafficking* involves buying and selling things such as drugs and weapons illegally, usually between countries.   **16.** internally displaced

Exercise 2

1. travel agency   **2.** package tour   **3.** independent travelers   **4.** visas   **5.** check in   **6.** coach class   **7.** disembark   **8.** mass tourism   **9.** all-inclusive   **10.** ecotourism   **11.** refugees   **12.** internally displaced   **13.** economic migrants   **14.** expatriates   **15.** culture shock   **16.** immigration   **17.** persona non grata   **18.** deported   **19.** checking in   **20.** excursion

Work (pages 102 – 103)

Exercise 1

1. applicant   **2.** A *wage* and a *salary* are both money you receive for doing a job, but the first is usually paid daily or weekly and the second is usually paid monthly   **3.** Repetitive strain injury (usually abbreviated to *RSI*)   **4.** fired   **5.** increment   **6.** A *blue-collar worker* does work that involves physical strength or skill with their hands (for example, in a factory or a mine) and a *white-collar worker* works in an office   **7.** False. It makes some of its workers *redundant* (= it gets rid of some of its workers) because it no longer needs them)   **8.** perks   **9.** *Sick building syndrome* is a medical condition that affects people who work in buildings where the air is not healthy   **10.** a steady job   **11.** False. When you *retire*, you stop working because you have reached a particular age. When you *resign*, you leave a job because (for example) you want a different job or because you are not happy with the company you are working for   **12.** service industries   **13.** No. Your work conditions are bad (for example, you might not have much job security, your place of work might be unhealthy or dangerous, etc.)   **14.** freelance (This can also be a verb: *to freelance*. The person who does this is called a *freelancer*)

Exercise 3

1. employees   **2.** unskilled   **3.** semi-skilled   **4.** blue-collar   **5.** manufacturing industries   **6.** white-collar   **7.** service industries   **8.** job security   **9.** steady job   **10.** hiring   **11.** firing   **12.** stress   **13.** demanding   **14.** unsociable hours   **15.** repetitive strain injury   **16.** salary   **17.** promotion   **18.** perks   **19.** incentive   **20.** increment / raise   **21.** sickness benefit   **22.** pension   **23.** self-employed

Mini topics

Friends and relations (pages 104 – 105)

Exercise 1

1. siblings / brother / sister   **2.** a lot in common / shared interests   **3.** see eye to eye / bond / fallen out   **4.** on good terms / boss / employee / supportive   **5.** admire or respect / close / acquaintance   **6.** amiable / related

Exercise 2

1. chemistry   **2.** True   **3.** buddy   **4.** False. If you *get on* with someone, you have a good relationship with them (we can also say *get along* with someone). If you *adore* someone, you love them very much   **5.** room mate   **6.** A nuclear family is a family that has a mother, father, and children living together. An extended family is a family that includes the parents, children, grandparents, and other relatives living together or very close to each other   **7.** True   **8.** partner   **9.** They have a very close relationship and spend all their time together (e.g., *My parents are inseparable*)   **10.** enemy   **11.** False. It is a formal word for a husband or wife.   **12.** inspiration

Health and exercise (page 105)

Exercise 1

1. in good shape / active / go jogging *or* go swimming / take up   **2.** Sedentary / overweight *or* obese (*fat* could be used in an informal context) / fast food (we also say *junk food*) / fat   **3.** unhealthy / put on weight / skin problems / balanced diet   **4.** slim / lifestyle / health club / keep fit *or* go swimming   **5.** look after / on a diet / cut down / give up   **6.** Obesity / obese *or* overweight (or, more informally, *fat*) / health problems / heart disease

Answer key

Movies and the theater (pages 106 – 107)

Exercise 1

1. science fiction *or* horror / soundtrack   **2.** comedy / funny *or* entertaining / acting *or* cast *or* plot *or* storyline   **3.** actress / actor *or* director / director *or* actor   **4.** horror *or* science fiction / frightening *or* terrifying / plot *or* storyline / special effects / screen / terrifying (not *frightening*, which cannot have *absolutely* before it)   **5.** play / musical / entertaining *or* exciting / cast / stars *or* actors   **6.** feel-good / audience / characters / atmosphere

Your home town (pages 107 – 108)

Exercise 1

1. nightlife   **2.** community spirit   **3.** character   **4.** pedestrianized   **5.** sports center   **6.** museum   **7.** neighborhood   **8.** neighbors   **9.** shopping mall   **10.** Healthcare   **11.** parks   **12.** amenities   **13.** job opportunities   **14.** renovated *or* rejuvenated   **15.** demolished   **16.** rejuvenated *or* renovated (generally, a *building* is renovated, and an *area* is rejuvenated)   **17.** historic   **18.** homelessness   **19.** street crime   **20.** traffic congestion   **21.** public transport   **22.** environment   **23.** rural   **24.** local customs

Learning languages (pages 108 – 109)

Exercise 1

1. progress   **2.** get by   **3.** dictionary   **4.** accent   **5.** pick up   **6.** bilingual   **7.** vocabulary   **8.** second language   **9.** competent   **10.** mother tongue (= first language)   **11.** pronunciation   **12.** practice   **13.** culture   **14.** grammar   **15.** fluent   **16.** communicate   **17.** native   **18.** rewarding